CW00421730

73

Learn Then Burn Teacher's Manual

cs

by Tim Stafford & Molly Meacham

Write Bloody Publishing
America's Independent Press

Long Beach, CA

writebloody.com

Stafford, Tim. Meacham, Molly.
1st edition.
ISBN: 978-1-935904-01-4

Interior Layout by Lea C. Deschenes
Cover Designed by Joshua Grieve
Proofread by Jennifer Roach
Edited by Tim Stafford and Molly Meacham
Type set in Bergamo and Aller

Printed in Tennessee, USA

Write Bloody Publishing
Long Beach, CA
Support Independent Presses
writebloody.com

To contact the authors or editors, send an email to writebloody@gmail.com

LEARN THEN BURN TEACHER'S MANUAL

SUPPLEMENTAL MATERIALS

LETTER TO THE TEACHERS

Hello, teachers.

If you are reading this, it means that you're a pretty rad teacher. It means that you care about what you teach your students and are willing to look at more unconventional ways to reach them. We hope that we can help. We're here to help you take your students beyond the basic, more traditional ways in which poetry is usually taught. And, yes, by "basic," we mean "boring."

Inside this book, you will find a variety of lessons, questions, and writing prompts to help foster an appreciation for poetry. These lessons were developed by classroom teachers who have been using spoken word as a way to hook our students. We have seen the power of poetry and have watched students who have never read a poem aloud go on to compete in a city-wide poetry slam. We have seen students from different racial, socioeconomic, and religious backgrounds come together to share their poetry with each other. The list goes on.

So now it's your turn. This book is a tool for you to use in your classroom. Only you know the intricacies of your classroom. Just because they worked in one classroom does not mean they will work in every classroom. Therefore, feel free to modify these lessons to suit your students' needs. Use the lessons as a supplement to an already active poetry unit. Add some of your own questions or writing prompts. Do what's best for your classroom. If you come up with something awesome, we'd love to hear about it so that we could share it with others.

Now go on with your bad self. You've got brains to feed.

Rock and/or roll,

Tim Stafford and Molly Meacham

OVERVIEW

As you go through these lessons, you will notice that some have questions and some do not. Most of the questions are specific to that poem. To help with the rest we have included a list of basic questions that can be used for not only the poems in this book, but for all poems in general.

These are some of the basic questions that may be addressed to help dig into the poems:

1. *Who is the speaker of the poem? What do you know about the speaker from what he/she/it says?*

2. *Who is the intended audience? How does that affect the course of the poem?*

3. *What is the subject addressed in the poem?*

4. *What is the purpose (or heart) of the poem?*

5. *How does the speaker's feeling toward the subject or audience affect the tone (the emotion) of the poem?*

Additional questions:

1. *What figurative language is used? Remember vocabulary: metaphor, simile, personification, animism, hyperbole, synecdoche, metonymy, allusion.*

2. *Does repetition or anaphora play a part?*

3. *How does cadence get created? Do any use form? Rhythm or meter?*

4. *What sounds affect the texture of the poem? Remember vocabulary: alliteration, assonance, consonance, onomatopoeia.*

"IN FRONT OF THE CLASS" BY BONAFIDE ROJAS

Repetition

Repetition is a technique that spans many poetic forms. It can appear in a sestina, a pantoum, or in the hook of a rap. Usually repetition is used to reinforce the poet's message. It can also give the poem a rhythm. In this poem, Bronx based poet Bonafide Rojas uses repetition to explain how he feels about the teaching profession.

Pre-Reading Prompt

If you were a teacher, what is the most important piece of advice you would give to your students?

After Reading Questions

1. *What words or phrases are repeated throughout this poem?*
   The phrases "I tell them," "tell them," and "let the page be" are repeated throughout the poem.

2. *What effect do these repeated words have on the reader?*
   The repeated phrases read like a list of demands. They come slowly at first but they start coming faster and faster as the poem goes along. It has a frantic effect on the reader.

3. *What message do you think the poet is trying to get across to the reader?*
   The message of this poem is that writing can give you all the things you need if you let it. It doesn't matter what background you come from. If you want it bad enough and are willing to work hard, you can achieve the unreachable.

After Reading Prompt

The poet asks his students, "What will be your legacy?" If you were to leave this school tomorrow and never come back, how would you want to be remembered by your peers? What have you done or what would you like to change to earn that legacy?

WORKSHEET: "IN FRONT OF THE CLASS" BY BONAFIDE ROJAS

Name: _____   Date: _____

Reading Questions

1. *What words or phrases are repeated throughout this poem?*

    _____

    _____

    _____

2. *What effect do these repeated words have on the reader?*

    _____

    _____

    _____

3. *What message do you think the poet is trying to get across to the reader?*

    _____

    _____

    _____

After Reading Prompt

The poet asks his students, "What will be your legacy?" If you were to leave this school tomorrow and never come back, how would you want to be remembered by your peers? What have you done or what would you like to change to earn that legacy?

"IGNITION" BY CRISTIN O'KEEFE APTOWICZ

Pre-reading or Writing Prompt:

Imagine the first time you tried something (G-rated, please). What was the reason? What were the sights, smells, tastes, and sounds that you remember around that experience?

Explain it to someone else so he or she would understand the feeling.

After Reading Questions:

1. *Why is the poem arranged the way it is?*
    The poem is mostly made of couplets. Each couplet refers to a certain scene. The scenes might be different but they are linked because they all have to do with something that happened "the first time." It isolates the images, but it allows the reader to read through the images quickly.

2. *Does the arrangement help or hinder the reading?*
    Student opinion; answers will vary.

3. *What do you notice about the punctuation? What effect does it have on reading?*
    The only punctuation is a comma in the last couplet. There is also no capitalization. This could be because the poet wants you to be able to read through it quickly. There is no punctuation to act as a road block. It indicates the pacing of the experience.

4. *Would the poem be different in first or third person?*
    Student opinion; answers will vary.

5. *What effect does it have on you to have the speaker talking to you?*
    The poet is making a connection with the reader whether they like it or not. The poet is forcing the reader to think about these experiences and make comparisons to their own similar experiences.

WORKSHEET: "IGNITION" BY CRISTIN O'KEEFE APTOWICZ

Name: _____   Date: _____

After Reading Questions:

1. *Why is the poem arranged the way it is?*

    _____

    _____

    _____

2. *Does the arrangement help or hinder the reading?*

    _____

    _____

    _____

3. *What do you notice about the punctuation? What effect does it have on reading?*

    _____

    _____

    _____

4. *Would the poem be different in first or third person?*

    _____

    _____

    _____

5. *What effect does it have on you to have the speaker talking to you?*

    _____

    _____

    _____

"HISTORY OF THE ARDENWOOD B-BOYS" BY JASON BAYANI

Personal Narrative

Narrative poems contain story elements such as plot, characters, conflict, and setting. It reads almost like a short story. This poem by the Bay Area poet Jason Bayani tells a story about himself and hip-hop. It is a personal narrative because these events are from his life and they are told from his perspective.

After Reading Questions

1. *From what perspective is this story being told?*
   First person perspective. There is distance between the speaker now and the action of the poem.

2. *What story elements are there in this poem?*
   There are characters, setting and conflict. The conflict occurs in the 7th stanza when the kids begin to fight.

3. *What makes this a poem and not a short story?*
   The way the text appears on the page. It is in stanzas instead of paragraphs. There are also poetic elements such as personification and simile.

4. *How does the story of his brother at the end of the poem fit into the narrative?*
   The last stanza about his brother reflects the first part of the poem. Just as he and his friends had to fight for what they wanted, so does his brother. Instead of proving something to the white kids at his school, however, his brother is proving something to himself.

5. *How would this poem be different if the perspective was switched?*
   The poem might not be as believable if the perspective was switched. By putting himself in the story, we get an insider's point of view. It also allows the reader to make more of a connection to the poet himself. If the perspective was switched, that connection might be lost.

Writing Prompt:

Have students begin a narrative poem with the line, "This is where I'm from."

Encourage students to write about positive memories. Encourage students to be specific in their choices and to not encompass their whole lives. They should pick no more than four specific memories that happen close to one another. If they can, have them pick one specific instance.

WORKSHEET: "HISTORY OF THE ARDENWOOD B-BOYS" BY JASON BAYANI

Name: _____   Date: _____

Questions

1. *From what perspective is this story being told?*

    _____

    _____

    _____

2. *What story elements are there in this poem?*

    _____

    _____

    _____

3. *What makes this a poem and not a short story?*

    _____

    _____

    _____

4. *How does the story of his brother at the end of the poem fit into the narrative?*

    _____

    _____

    _____

5. *How would this poem be different if the perspective was switched?*

    _____

    _____

    _____

Writing Prompt:

Begin a narrative poem with the line, "This is where I'm from." Write about positive memories. Be specific in your choices and do not encompass your whole life. You should pick no more than four specific memories that happen close to one another. If you can, pick one specific instance.

"WATER GUN" BY BUDDY WAKEFIELD

In his poem "Water Gun," former World Slam Champion Buddy Wakefield uses purposeful contradictions and colloquialisms to get his message across. He also uses a lot of clichés but flips the interpretation. Before reading you should review the meanings of some of these phrases:

"*foot in my mouth,*" "*making a mountain out of a molehill,*" "*take the wind out of sails,*" "*wearing out a welcome,*" and "*backed into a corner.*"

You can write them on the board or pass out different phrases to students to see if they can come up with the meanings on their own.

After Reading Questions:

1. *What sayings have you heard before? How are they different?*
   They should recognize the colloquialisms that were gone over at the beginning of the class. They should see flips in the clichés like "You approached me like a molehill in the hour of my mountain."

2. *What sort of images stand out in the poem?*
   Student opinion; answers will vary.

3. *What unusual actions are revealed? Look at the verbs and subjects acting it out.*
   Student opinion; answers will vary. "Like a cocky lion struttin' in the mouth of a whale."

4. *How does the poet use contradictions to paint a picture of the audience?*
   Student opinion; answers will vary.

5. *How does the poet flip the cliché of a mountain and a molehill to set off the nature of the relationship?*
   A molehill is something small. Typically we make something huge out of something small. He uses the shift in size to indicate the almost sneak attack of the "you."

6. *What is the speaker like? Who is the audience?*
   Student opinion; answers will vary. But the audience (the "you") is an ex to the speaker.

"TAMBOURINE! TAMBOURINE! TAMBOURINE! TAMBOURINE!" BY SHANNY JEAN MANY

Mood

How does a poem make you feel? It depends on the poet. Some will give you a sense of joy and others will make you feel depressed. The feeling you get from a poem is called the mood. The mood a poet creates depends on word choice, repetition, and use of poetic devices, to name a few. Take a look at the poem "TAMBOURINE! TAMBOURINE! TAMBOURINE! TAMBOURINE!" by Shanny Jean.

Reading Quesions

1. *Ask students to describe what it's like to be in a bad mood. More importantly, ask them what puts them in a bad mood. If you want to keep it positive, ask them what it's like to be in a good mood.*

2. *Now ask students if they've ever had strong feelings about characters or situations in a story or poem they read. Try to use an example from a text previously used in class.*

3. *Tell them that they had those feeling because the author has created a mood in their writing. They want you to feel a certain way about a situation or character so they use techniques such as repetition, word choice, and poetic devices to push you in that direction.*

4. *Now that they know what mood is, you can pass out "TAMBOURINE!" by Shanny Jean Maney-Magnuson.*

5. *Ask students to read through the poem silently and to try to detect the mood.*

6. *After they have done so, ask someone to read it aloud and make sure they emphasize the parts with exclamation points. You may want to give them permission to shout the parts that are capitalized.*

7. *Now ask students to describe the mood and to give specific reasons (repetition, similar words, punctuation, etc).*

8. *Some questions you might want to ask are: How does the poet want you to feel when you read this poem? How does punctuation affect the poem? How does the repetition add to the overall mood? Why do you think the poet included words such as "FLAVOR CRYSTALS" and "MONKEYBRAIN" in this poem?*

Writing Prompt:

Mood is created by the poet. Have students pick a mood and write a poem that shows it. Encourage students to think of something besides a good or bad mood. Why not a poem with a relaxed, crazy, excited, or ominous mood? Make sure they use word choice, repetition, or other poetic devices to help them write.

"THE NAT TURNER CHASE MOVIE PITCH" BY IDRIS GOODWIN

Pre-Reading Questions

1. *Who can describe their favorite chase movie or chase scene?*

2. *Who was Nat Turner? (He was a slave who led a rebellion in Virginia in 1831. After the rebellion, he went into hiding where he was ultimately caught and executed.)*

After Reading Questions

1. *Who is the speaker of this poem?*
    The speaker is someone who is trying to make a movie about Nat Turner. The repetition makes it seem like this person is excited about the project and is trying to get a producer to buy into the idea.

2. *How does this movie pitch differ from the actual story of Nat Turner?*
    Nat Turner was never in a desert. He was in Virginia. There were also no helicopters involved in the chase. The Nat Turner story also never mentions him getting advice from wildlife.

3. *Why do you think he made those changes?*
    Student answers will vary.

4. *What could the passing on to the coyote and the rattlesnake symbolize?*
    A human is mortal. Everyone has to die but their influence can live on forever if the story is passed along. Nat's story is passed on to animals that cannot be caught. This means that his story and influence cannot be caught. His influence is still being passed along.

Writing Prompt:

Think of historical figures you have already learned about. Pitch a movie about their life. Will it be an action movie, chase movie, comedy, drama, or horror? Write it as if you are presenting the idea to a producer.

WORKSHEET: "THE NAT TURNER CHASE MOVIE PITCH" BY IDRIS GOODWIN

Name: _____   Date: _____

After Reading Questions:

1. *Who is the speaker of this poem?*

_____

_____

_____

2. *How does this movie pitch differ from the actual story of Nat Turner?*

_____

_____

_____

3. *Why do you think he made those changes?*

_____

_____

_____

4. *What could the passing on to the coyote and the rattlesnake symbolize?*

_____

_____

_____

Writing Prompt:

Think of historical figures you have already learned about. Pitch a movie about their life. Will it be an action movie, chase movie, comedy, drama, or horror? Write it as if you are presenting the idea to a producer.

"YOUR FOSSIL IS IN THE SHAPE OF MY MOUTH" BY SARAH MORGAN

Pantoum

A pantoum is a form developed in Malayan literature. It is a poem made up of four-line stanzas. There is no limit on how many stanzas there can be. The poem contains repeated lines that connect from stanza to stanza. Lines 2 and 4 are taken from one stanza and repeated as lines 1 and 3 in the next.

_____ Line 1

_____ Line 2

_____ Line 3

_____ Line 4

_____ Line 5—same as line 2

_____ Line 6

_____ Line 7—same as line 4

_____ Line 8

_____ Line 9—same as line 6

_____ Line 10

_____ Line 11—same as line 8

_____ Line 12

Pre-Reading Questions

1. *If you have already worked on repetition, ask your students to tell you some reasons why poets use repetition.*

2. *Tell students that they will be reading a pantoum.*

3. *Do not explain what a pantoum is. Have them try to figure out the pattern as they read and re-read the poem.*

4. *Ask students if anyone has figured out the pattern.*

5. *Once you have heard answers from other students, explain in detail what a pantoum is.*

6. Pass out the "Pantoum Organizer" located in the back of the book.

7. Explain to them that they will be writing their own so they need to think carefully about which lines they want repeated.

8. Have them start with the line, "In my dreams we were. . . ." and leave the rest up to them.

"THE HANGED MAN TALKS ABOUT TRANSITION" BY MARTY MCCONNELL

Sestina

A sestina is a form that is fixed on the number six. There are six stanzas with six unrhymed lines. The words at the end of each line reappear in different order from stanza to stanza. The poem is completed by a three line stanza called a tercet that uses all six end words.

If you use "The Hanged Man Talks About Transition" as an example, you will see how this form is utilized. To help students understand, use the following guide for the end words:

A—   taut

B—   cleave

C—   body

D—   self

E—   known

F—   trans

This is a good time to ask your students about the author's purpose. Ask them about the reasoning behind the repeated words. Why did the poet use those six words? Do the words change meaning throughout the poem?

After discussing the poem, use the "Sestina Organizer" to help students create their own sestinas.

Other examples of a sestina:

"Sestina" by Elizabeth Bishop, "Sestina" by Dante Alighieri

"ODE TO THE BOOM BOX" BY KEVIN COVAL

Ode

Odes traditionally have a complex metrical structure, more than one stanza (creating sections that break down into the strophe, antistrophe, and epode), and a rhyme scheme, but the modern ode doesn't have much of a form. One element that stays the same is that the ode addresses a specific object, person, or theme. An ode is usually written to glorify or exalt the subject of the poem.

"Ode to the boom box" by Kevin Coval is a modern take on the ode. Kevin Coval has chosen to glorify an object that may seem simple to some but which has had a profound impact on his life.

After Reading Questions

1. *Of all the objects in the world, why do you think a poet would choose to write an ode for a boom box?*
   This poet probably really likes listening to music. The boom box provides the music and the music provides entertainment, education, and company. The poet talks about spending hours making tapes so you know that he spent a large amount of time with the boom box.

2. *What lines of the poem seem to glorify the boom box?*
   "The possible voice at constant watch," "the speak/that quiets and saves before sleep," "company and accompaniment/before Nintendo," "activating our imagination."

3. *Why does the poet include the epigraph from the King James Bible at the beginning of the poem?*
   The poet compares the voices he hears coming from the boom box to that of God. This could be because the voices he hears are creating new worlds that the poet has never seen. The boom box has become such a large part of his life that it seems like he can't live without it.

Writing Prompt:

An ode is a good form to use especially with young writers who may not have written much poetry before. They don't have to worry about counting lines or a rhyming pattern. Have your students find a person or personal object that might seem silly to some but which is extremely important to them. Have them write an ode for that person or object that uses details to describe its importance.

WORKSHEET: "ODE TO THE BOOMBOX" BY KEVIN COVAL

Name: _____   Date: _____

Questions

1. *Of all the objects in the world, why do you think a poet would choose to write an ode for a boom box?*

   _____

   _____

   _____

2. *What lines of the poem seem to glorify the boom box?*

   _____

   _____

   _____

3. *Why does the poet include the epigraph from the King James Bible at the beginning of the poem?*

   _____

   _____

   _____

Writing Prompt:

Think of a person or personal object that might seem silly to some but which is extremely important to you. Write an ode for that person or object that uses details and figurative language to show its importance.

"HIPS FOR THE HOP" BY DAN SULLIVAN

Poem for Unsung Heroes

In his poem "Hips for the Hop," Dan Sullivan displays the impact women have had on hip hop music throughout its history. This poem brings the opportunity to discuss roles of women in popular music with your class. Hip hop (as well as heavy metal, punk rock, alternative, etc) is often seen as a male-dominated genre with women relegated to lesser roles. This poem sheds some light on female contributions that are often overlooked.

It always helps to have music and pictures of the females artists mentioned in this poem.

Pre-Reading Questions:

1. *Ask students to list as many rappers as they can.*

2. *Have students share and create a master list in a visible area of the room. (In most cases, the list is predominantly, if not totally, male-dominated.)*

3. *After you have created the list, ask students to look at the list and see if they can come up with anything most of the people on the list have in common (stylistically similar, from the same area, on the same label, etc.).*

4. *If no students mention that they are all male, ask them, "Where are the females?" Students will manage to name a couple of female emcees but you most often hear about females being the back-up dancers or back-up singers for male rappers.*

5. *Pass out copies of "Hips for the Hop."*

After Reading Questions:

6. *Ask your students if they have ever heard of any of the women referenced. Most times they know a couple but most they have never been exposed to.*

7. *Ask your students, "Why do you think you've never heard of these women before?", "Are their contributions less important than their male counterparts?", "If not, why do the males get most of the credit?", "Could these women be considered unsung heroes?"*

8. *From here it depends on the responses of the class and how far you want to take it. Students usually have a lot to say about the subject so it is best to reserve enough time to have a thorough discussion. The comments and questions from students will begin to fuel the lesson. Make sure that you use the questions to keep them on track.*

Writing Prompts

Choose a group that deserves praise (usual or unusual): sleepwalkers, janitors, debaters, stepmothers, etc. Make a list of actions that group would accomplish and put them into a poem for your "unsung heroes".

"ROUGH DRAFT" BY BILLY TUGGLE

Tone

Tone is the attitude a poet takes toward the subject of their poem. The tone of the poem will change depending on how they feel about the subject. In his poem "Rough Draft," the 2008 Chicago Slam Champion Billy Tuggle guides us on a journey through his high school years as a graffiti artist.

Before Reading Questions:

There is a lot of debate about the merits of graffiti. Some people view it as art while others view it as vandalism. Ask students what their opinion of graffiti is. Is it one or the other? Can it be both?

Explain to students what tone is. Then tell them "We are going to read a poem about graffiti. I want you to think about tone as we read. I want you to tell me what the poet's tone is toward graffiti."

After Reading Questions:

1. *What is the tone the poet takes toward graffiti?*
    The poet understands that his artwork is illegal. He also understands that he is at risk from other artists who want to bring him down. However, he is willing to accept responsibility for his actions. He shows us how graffiti can convey a positive message. It might be flawed, but it is still a powerful art form.

2. *In the second stanza, Billy refers to himself as a "spray-can sniper." Why?*
    Graffiti artists and snipers are similar in nature. They both work secretly and quickly. They try not to draw any unnecessary attention to themselves. They do their job and get out, only a graffiti artist uses spray paint instead of bullets.

3. *Where is this taking place? What clues can you use to back up your answer?*
    This is most likely taking place in an urban setting. He mentions "crowding the moves of the masses," which makes one think of huge crowds clogging a downtown area or transit hub. He also mentions that he ran subway tracks, tunnels, and station platforms. If he was on foot, he had to be close to those places.

4. *Do you agree with his view of graffiti? Why or why not?*
    Student answers will vary.

WORKSHEET: "ROUGH DRAFT" BY BILLY TUGGLE

Name: _____   Date: _____

Tone

Tone is the attitude a poet takes toward the subject of their poem. The tone of the poem will change depending on how they feel about the subject. In his poem "Rough Draft," the 2008 Chicago Slam Champion Billy Tuggle guides us on a journey through his high school years as a graffiti artist.

1. *What is the tone the poet takes toward graffiti?*

   _____

   _____

   _____

2. *In the second stanza, Billy refers to himself as a "spray-can sniper." Why?*

   _____

   _____

   _____

3. *Where is this taking place? What clues can you use to back up your answer?*

   _____

   _____

   _____

4. *Do you agree with his view of graffiti? Why or why not?*

   _____

   _____

   _____

"UNDERDOG" BY BEN BUTTER

Off-Rhyme

An off-rhyme (also known as slant or oblique rhyme) is a rhyme that is not perfect. The rhyming words might sound similar due to the consonant and vowel sounds, but they don't rhyme completely (such as "past" and "pants"). The following poem is full of off-rhymes as well as comp rhymes.

Pre-Reading Questions:

1. *Ask students to define or give examples of an underdog.*

2. *Ask some of the students to explain how their example qualifies as an underdog.*

3. *Collect the answers because students will use them for the writing prompt.*

4. *Tell the students that they will be reading a poem about underdogs that uses off-rhyme.*

5. *Explain to them what an off-rhyme is. Ask the students to be on the lookout for off-rhymes as they read the poem.*

After Reading Questions:

1. *What are some of the lines that had off-rhymes?*
   Most of the lines from the first and third stanzas are off-rhymes.

2. *What effect does the use of off-rhyme have on this poem?*
   The rhyming itself gives a rhythm or flow to the poem. The off-rhymes create a sense of unpredictability. A perfect rhyme is easy to predict but the off-rhymes keep you guessing as to what word will come after.

3. *Who is the underdog in this poem? Why are they an underdog?*
   The underdog in this poem is an original. They don't go with the trends or try to be cool. They just try to be true to themselves. They are underdogs because we live in a world that puts a lot of pressure on young people to dress, speak, and act a certain way. Someone who does not bow to that pressure and perseveres despite the odds can be considered an underdog.

Writing Prompt:

Look at the list of underdogs that were collected at the beginning of class. Pick one of those to write a poem about. Your poem has to have parts that rhyme including perfect and off-rhymes. You do not have to rhyme the whole thing, but you can if you want.

WORKSHEET: "UNDERDOG" BY BEN BUTTER

Name: _____   Date: _____

Off-Rhyme

An off-rhyme is a rhyme that is not perfect. The rhyming words might sound similar but they don't rhyme perfectly (such as "past" and "pants"). They have similar consonant sounds but are not perfect.

1. What are some of the lines that had off-rhymes?

_____

_____

_____

2. What effect does the use of off-rhyme have on this poem?

_____

_____

_____

3. Who is the underdog in this poem? Why are they an underdog?

_____

_____

_____

Writing Prompt:

Look at the list of underdogs that were collected at the beginning of class. Pick one of those to write a poem about. Your poem has to have parts that rhyme including perfect and off-rhymes. You do not have to rhyme the whole thing, but you can if you want.

"NELLY AND HER DREAM" BY JOEL CHMARA

Symbolism

A symbol is an object or person that has its own meaning but also represents something more. Poets often use symbolism to create a link between the subject of the poem and the emotion or meaning they want you to take from the poem.

In the poem "Nelly and her Dream," Joel Chmara uses the mythical sea monster of Loch Ness as his symbol. Ask your students the following questions and see if they can figure out what Nelly symbolizes.

1. *What might Nelly symbolize?*
   Nelly is a lonely, solitary creature seeking out another like her. This could mean that she symbolizes anybody who is looking for friendship or for someone like them that they could relate to.

2. *What parts of the poem can you use to back up your answer?*
   The saddest day was when she realized she was the only one. She has searched the whole lake, hoping there were others searching for her.

3. *Why would the poet compare Nelly to the parents of a missing child?*
   Both have dedicated their lives to searching for a specific person. They have poured everything they have into the search. They are both at the point when they are beginning to lose hope.

4. *Why does the poet say, "For us to call this lonely soul a monster/ Is truly unfair"?*
   A monster is a being that is frightening, ugly, or misunderstood. Although she might be frightening to some, all she is trying to do is find someone like herself.

Writing Prompt:

Write a poem from the point of view of Nelly. What would she have to say about being the last of her kind?

Or

Write a poem from the point of view of another mysterious creature like Bigfoot, Chupacabra, or Sasquatch. What would they have to say about being the last of their kind?

WORKSHEET: "NELLY AND HER DREAM OF FRIENDSHIP" BY JOEL CHMARA

Name: _____   Date: _____

Symbolism

A symbol is an object or person that has its own meaning but also represents something more. Poets often use symbolism to create a link between the subject of the poem and the emotion or meaning they want you to take from the poem.

1. What might Nelly symbolize?

_____

_____

_____

2. What parts of the poem can you use to back up your answer?

_____

_____

_____

3. Why would the poet compare Nelly to the parents of a missing child?

_____

_____

_____

4. Why does the poet say, "For us to call this lonely soul a monster/ Is truly unfair"?

_____

_____

_____

Writing Prompt:

Write a poem from the point of view of Nelly (or other mysterious creatures like Bigfoot or Chupacabra). What would she have to say about being the last of her kind?

"LONELINESS" BY REGGIE ELDRIDGE

The topic of loneliness is something that most teenagers can relate to. They are at an age when they are trying to fit in and trying to find their identity. Friends come and go, and sometimes a kid feels left out. Tampa-based poet Reggie Eldridge writes about loneliness and expresses his feelings about it by using specific word choices. Pay attention to how he uses those words to "show" rather then "tell."

Pre-Reading Questions:

1. *Is being lonely a good or bad thing? Can it be both?*

2. *Is there a difference between being alone and being lonely?*

After Reading Questions:

1. *What is the poet's attitude toward loneliness?*
   The poet does not like the loneliness. The overall mood is ominous because he says that he can't escape when the nightmares call him.

2. *What words does the poet use to express his attitude?*
   Ghost, fading, absence, silence, infertile, nightmares.

3. *Who is the poet talking to in this poem?*
   The poet might be speaking to the loneliness. By comparing himself to a ghost, he makes it seem as if he is empty. Maybe he is so empty and alone that the only thing he can communicate with is his loneliness. He can't escape because he is hopeless and has nobody to help him.

WORKSHEET: "LONELINESS" BY REGGIE ELDRIDGE

Name: _____   Date: _____

Questions:

1. *What is the poet's attitude toward loneliness?*

_____

_____

_____

_____

_____

_____

2. *What words does the poet use to express his attitude?*

_____

_____

_____

_____

_____

_____

3. *Who is the poet talking to in this poem?*

_____

_____

_____

_____

_____

_____

"POX" BY GEOFF TRENCHARD

Pre-Reading Prompt:

Think of small events in your life that helped make you who you are (nothing bigger than a broken bone or getting braces). How did they shape you?

After Reading Questions:

1. *How do the stanzas form a progression for the poet?*
   The stanzas build up to a climax. Each stanza is more intense than the last until the final stanza. The poet has progressed through the breakouts but still remembers what it was like.

2. *What tense does the poet use?*
   The poet describes things that happened in the past tense. However, he intertwines some things in the past tense with some from the present tense. It makes you think that although these things happened in the past, they are still very much a part of him.

3. *How distant is the speaker from the breakouts?*
   He mentions its happening when he was thirteen years old, but it took a while to get the breakouts under control. It seems like a lot of time has passed but he writes so vividly about it that it could've been happening weeks ago rather than years.

Writing Prompt:

Use either the small event used in "pre-reading" or another small ordeal.

Use at least one stanza that uses anaphora (repetition of a word or phrase) with the words "I remember."

WORKSHEET: "POX" BY GEOFF TRENCHARD

Name: _____   Date: _____

Questions

1. *How do the stanzas form a progression for the poet?*

   _____

   _____

   _____

   _____

2. *What tense does the poet use?*

   _____

   _____

   _____

   _____

3. *How distant is the speaker from the breakouts?*

   _____

   _____

   _____

   _____

Writing Prompt:

Use either the small event used in "pre-reading" or another small ordeal.

Use at least one stanza that uses anaphora (repetition of a word or phrase) with the words "I remember."

"SOUND OF REVOLUTION" BY ED MABREY

Revolution/Change

In his poem "Sound of Revolution," 2007 Indy World Slam Champion Ed Mabrey argues that revolution exists in small, personal actions that occur daily. This poem provides an opportunity to discuss the way people make change in the world and how little actions can be revolutionary.

Pre-Reading Questions:

1. *Ask your students, "What is a revolution?"*

2. *If they can't come up with a clear definition, ask them the reasons behind the American Revolution, French Revolution, or the American Slave Revolts.*

3. *Ask your students to describe the characteristics and qualities of a revolutionary. Most often you will get descriptions of militant people with weapons.*

4. *Create a list of those characteristics and create a character map as a class.*

5. *Ask students to keep this character map in mind as you read this poem.*

After Reading Questions:

1. *Compare the character map to the people in this poem.*

2. *Ask your students, "Do these characters match the character map we created?"*

3. *"How are they alike/different?"*

4. *"Are these people revolutionaries?"*

5. *Allow time for discussion as whether they are or not.*

6. *At this point introduce the quotation, "Every journey of a thousand miles begins with a single step." – Lao Tzu*

7. *Ask them to consider this quotation and how it applies to the people in this poem.*

Writing Prompt:

What's your Revolution?

Consider the actions of the people in this poem and the quotation by Lao Tzu. If small actions can lead to great changes, what actions of yours can be considered revolutionary? What changes do you think can come from them?

"YE MODERN WOMAN" BY DASHA KELLY

Dasha Kelly is a slam poet from Milwaukee, Wisconsin. In her poem she issues a warning to modern women. This lesson is designed to make students think about words they associate with certain groups of people and how those words can be interpreted by others.

Pre-Reading Questions:

1. *Have your students create definitions for strong and able.*

2. *Ask them, "What textures and traditions are tied to those words?"*

After Reading Questions:

1. *How does Kelly use those definitions as positives and negatives?*
   In the poem, being strong is good because it is the "iron girds/inside our children's prayers." Being strong and able is negative though because that is what "wheels peasants and slaves to markets."

2. *How does the audience affect how the words are used?*
   The poem implies that men have a picture of what a woman should be. She uses words such as "fair," "delicate," and "trinkets." These are not words one associates with someone who is strong and able, therefore they are less desirable. From the child's perspective though, they need someone strong and able. No matter how hard you try to comfort a child, they will almost always ask for their mother.

3. *Are there words similarly difficult and good for men? Why or why not?*
   Student answers will vary.

Additional Reading:

"Phenomenal Woman" by Maya Angelou

WORKSHEET: "YE MODERN WOMAN" BY DASHA KELLY

Name: _____   Date: _____

Questions:

1. In your own words, write the definitions of the words "strong" and "able."

   _____

   _____

   _____

   _____

2. How does Kelly use those definitions as positives and negatives?

   _____

   _____

   _____

   _____

3. How does the audience affect how the words are used?

   _____

   _____

   _____

   _____

4. Are there words similarly difficult and good for men? Why or why not?

   _____

   _____

   _____

   _____

"DANCING IN THE RAIN WITH ANNIE" BY DANE KUTTLER

Creating Imagery With Action

In this poem, Seattle-based poet Dane Kuttler uses vivid verbs to illustrate a specific moment. Use the following lesson to get your students writing about action. This lesson would be good to use as part of an alliteration unit.

Reading Questions:

1. *Ask your students, "How do verbs create imagery?"*

2. *Tell them the title of this poem and ask them to think of verbs that would go with the title.*

3. *Collect the answers and then read the poem.*

4. *Ask students to reread the poem and examine it for moments of action.*

5. *Ask them, "How does the verb usage in the poem help create the momentum and situation of the piece?"*

6. *They should be able to identify that the verbs create a playful, almost rebellious situation.*

7. *Remind students of alliteration.*

8. *Have students go back and identify the alliteration in this poem.*

9. *Ask them, "How do sounds found in the verbs (alliteration, assonance, consonance) play into the concept of dancing in rain?"*

10. *Possible answers could be that the repetition of the sounds creates a rhythm much like the sound of constantly falling raindrops. Rhythm is also what is needed for dancing.*

Writing Prompt:

Have your students make a list of favorite verbs. Share with the class or with small groups and add to the list. Look at the list and have your students pick an action that is associated with the verbs on their list. They have to write a poem about a specific action (sports, brushing their teeth, listening to music, riding the bus, etc.) that uses as many verbs on their list as possible.

"THE BICYCLE" BY MARY FONS

What is a poem supposed to look like? That is the question you are going to pose to your students with this lesson. "The Bicycle" by Mary Fons looks a little different than most poems in this book because of her manipulation of the structure and use of punctuation.

Pre-reading Questions

1. *What is a poem supposed to look like?*

2. *How does the space a poem uses affect the reading of it?*

After Reading:

1. *What do you notice about the space and structure of the poem?*
   The stanzas look like paragraphs. There aren't any line breaks. Instead, she has inserted many backslashes. It's packed together whereas most poems are broken up and have more space.

2. *How does Mary Fons use the backslashes and proper line breaks to create momentum?*
   The backslashes look like they are in places most poets would break the line. By not breaking the line it allows the reader to keep moving through the poem. It doesn't slow down. The parts that do have proper line breaks allow the reader to take a breath before switching the scene a bit.

3. *How does the subject of the bicycle work with the structure?*
   When you ride a bike, you always start slowly. You have to press the pedals down and gain momentum before you can coast down the street at full speed. Much like a bicycle, this poem starts slowly with a couple of short lines. As the poem goes on, it gains momentum and moves quickly. The more lines the poet gets down, the faster she pedals. If you stop a bicycle too fast, you'll flip over the handlebars. This is why the poet eases to the finish with a shorter three-line stanza.

Writing Prompt:

Write a poem about travel.

Why do we travel? How do we travel? What's more important, the journey or the destination? Think about these questions as you create your own poem about traveling. Play with the lines and line breaks. Play with the shape of the poem to reflect your mode of transportation.

WORKSHEET: "THE BICYCLE" BY MARY FONS

Name: _____   Date: _____

Questions:

1. *What do you notice about the space and structure of the poem?*

   _____

   _____

   _____

   _____

2. *How does Mary Fons use the backslashes and proper line breaks to create momentum?*

   _____

   _____

   _____

   _____

3. *How does the subject of the bicycle work with the structure?*

   _____

   _____

   _____

   _____

Writing Prompt:

Write a poem about travel.

Why do we travel? How do we travel? What's more important, the journey or the destination? Think about these questions as you create your own poem about traveling. Play with the lines and line breaks. Play with the shape of the poem to reflect your mode of transportation.

"SOMETHING THAT LIVES BETWEEN THE TWO" BY JOAQUIN ZIHUATANEJO

2008 Individual World Poetry Slam Champion and 2009 World Cup of Poetry Slam Champion Joaquin Zihuatanejo is a teaching poet from Dallas, Texas. In this poem, he shows glimpses of his teaching, poetic, and family life.

Reading Questions:

1. *Why is it better to find poetry in a place you don't expect rather than a place you do expect?*
   When you find something you don't expect, you are surprised. It also provides hope. If you can find poetry in one unexpected place, you can probably find poetry anywhere. You just have to be willing to look for it.

2. *Does the poet give any example of poetry being found in unexpected places?*
   The poet has turned sneaking tacos into a classroom into a part of his poem. He also describes an interaction between his parents that seems mundane to most but ends up being the catalyst behind this poem.

3. *What does it mean to be "something that lives between the two"?*
   The poet is a product of his parents. Instead of taking after both, he has adopted traits of each. At times he might be fire but at the same time he has the power within to extinguish the flames before they become an inferno.

Writing Prompt: Finding Poetry in Unexpected Places

Create a list of all the different places you enter at school. This includes classrooms, hallways, cafeterias, and, yes, even bathrooms. Choose one of those places to write a poem about. Here is the tricky part: you can't say what room it is. You are going to show what room it is by using descriptive details and figurative language. The reader is going to have to use the clues you've provided to figure it out.

Extra Credit

Joaquin mentions four poets in the second stanza. Ask students to look up one of the poets and present a brief biography as well as poem samples of the poet. If you want to go further, ask them to write a research paper on one of the poets.

WORKSHEET: "SOMETHING THAT LIVES BETWEEN THE TWO" BY JOAQUIN ZIHUATANEJO

Name: _____   Date: _____

Questions:

1. *Why is it better to find poetry in a place you don't expect rather than a place you do expect?*

   _____

   _____

   _____

   _____

2. *Does the poet give any example of poetry being found in unexpected places?*

   _____

   _____

   _____

   _____

3. *What does it mean to be "something that lives between the two"?*

   _____

   _____

   _____

   _____

Writing Prompt: Finding Poetry in Unexpected Places

Create a list of all the different places you enter at school. This includes classrooms, hallways, cafeterias, and, yes, even bathrooms. Choose one of those places to write a poem about. Here is the tricky part: you can't say what room it is. You are going to show what room it is by using descriptive details and figurative language. The reader is going to have to use the clues you've provided to figure it out.

"WEAKS OF SILENCE" BY SARAH LIHZ

Omaha poet Sarah Lihz writes about the relationship between herself and her sister in her poem "Weaks of Silence". Notice how she uses allusion and metaphor to show the reader what is going on.

Pre-reading Questions:

1. *Who have you wanted to connect with, really communicate with?*

2. *Why is it hard? What could help?*

After Reading Questions:

1. *What do you understand about the speaker's sister from the poem?*

2. *How does nature represent their relationship? Is the nature positive or negative in the poem?*

3. *What does the allusion of the rock rolling away from her sister's mouth do for the poem? Why did the poet use that allusion?*

4. *What is the significance of the title?*

Writing Prompt:

Have there been moments where words don't work? What does that feel like? What does it look like? What do you associate with that?

And

When communication (even in silence) works, what images do you associate with that? How do you appear to the other person?

"PHONE WIRES" BY NOVA VENERABLE

Pre-reading Question:

Have you ever lost contact with someone you were once close to? What happened?

After Reading Questions:

1. *How do the phone wires symbolize the relationship between the speaker and her father?*

2. *Why does she repeat the line "Over, Under, Over, Under"?*

3. *Do you think she should feel guilty about lying to her father? Why or why not?*

4. *How does the speaker feel about her father?*

5. *How does the speaker feel toward her mother?*

6. *How do you think the father feels about the speaker?*

Writing Prompt:

Write a letter to someone you've lost touch with. Explain to them your reasons for losing touch. Or if someone has lost touch with you, write them a letter to let them know how it has affected you.

"NEVER" BY JACOB SAM-LA ROSE

"Never" by London-based poet Jacob Sam-La Rose is a poem told from the first person perspective. The speaker of the poem is talking about someone, but his or her identity is never revealed. Students will have to find clues in the text to infer who that person is.

1. *In your opinion, how do you think the speaker of the poem feels about the person they are talking about?*
   The poet seems indifferent about the subject. It's almost as if he is casually running down a list. This could be because he doesn't really know the subject at all. On one hand he has missed out on good things, but he has also avoided the bad.

2. *Who do you think the poet is talking about?*
   The poet is most likely talking about his father.

3. *What evidence from the text or real-life examples can you use to back up your answer?*
   All of the things he is talking about are things that sons typically do with their fathers. He also refers to the subject as "him" so we know that it is some sort of male figure. It has to be a relative because only a relative would have hands that looked the same as his.

4. *What has happened to the subject of the poem?*
   The subject has not been in the poet's life for a very long time, long enough that the poet cannot remember his voice. He might have left his family or passed away when the poet was just a child.

5. *If you had to rename this poem, what would you change it to?*
   Student answers will vary.

WORKSHEET: "NEVER" BY JACOB SAM-LA ROSE

Name: _____   Date: _____

Questions

1. *In your opinion, how do you think the speaker of the poem feels about the person they are talking about?*

    _____

    _____

    _____

2. *Who do you think the poet is talking about?*

    _____

    _____

    _____

3. *What evidence from the text or real-life examples can you use to back up your answer?*

    _____

    _____

    _____

4. *What has happened to the subject of the poem?*

    _____

    _____

    _____

5. *If you had to rename this poem, what would you change it to? Why?*

    _____

    _____

    _____

"UNTITLED" BY JESSICA DISU

In her poem "Untitled," Chicago based poet/MC Jessica Disu tells us about her grandmother. She uses repetition and simile to paint a picture of their unique relationship.

Start off by asking the class to write about the following prompt:

Write about a time that you changed your opinion about someone from a negative opinion to a positive one. What caused the change?

Reading Questions:

1. *Why does the poet refer to her grandmother as a robot?*
    The grandmother does not have any sympathy for her grandchildren. They have chores to do, and if they don't do them, they will be punished. Maybe she has to be so hard on her grandchildren because there are so many of them and she has to work late. She doesn't have the time to nurture them.

2. *Why does the poet refer to herself and the rest of the grandchildren as zombies?*
    One reason is that they are forced to wake up early to do their chores. They are moving slowly and aren't even fully awake. Another reason could be that a zombie is the opposite of a robot. This helps emphasize the differences between grandchild and grandparent.

3. *What do you think the significance is of the two food-related similes in this poem ("made our stomachs turn like machines," and "cling to her like collard greens")?*
    The first simile occurs at the beginning of the poem when the poet's relationship with her grandmother is not going well. To match the relationship, the poet has included a simile that has a negative connotation. Later in the poem, the poet has come to an understanding with her grandmother and their relationship improves. To reflect that, she uses the simile about collard greens, which emphasizes the positive change.

4. *Why do you think their relationship has improved? What has brought about the change?*
    It could be simply that people change with age. Perhaps the poet has proved herself to her grandmother so she now gets the respect she wants. Maybe now the poet understands why her grandmother was so hard on her.

Writing Prompt:

Write a response to this poem from the point of view of the grandmother that explains why she isn't her granddaughter's biggest fan.

WORKSHEET: "UNTITLED" BY JESSICA DISU

Name: _____   Date: _____

Reading Questions:

1. *Why does the poet refer to her grandmother as a robot?*

   _____

   _____

   _____

2. *Why does the poet refer to herself and the rest of the grandchildren as zombies?*

   _____

   _____

   _____

3. *What do you think the significance is of the two food-related smiles in this poem ("made our stomachs turn like machines," and "cling to her like collard greens")?*

   _____

   _____

   _____

4. *Why do you think their relationship has improved? What has brought about the change?*

   _____

   _____

   _____

Writing Prompt:

Write a response to this poem from the point of view of the grandmother that explains why she isn't her granddaughter's biggest fan.

"PAIN SUITE" BY CHARLES ELLIK

Haiku

Haiku is a poem made of only three lines: the first line has five syllables, the second line has seven syllables, and the third line has five syllables. Traditionally, a haiku addresses nature and everyday, simple subjects. It originated in Japan and is a great example of "less is more." The poet has very little amount of space to capture an image so they have to choose what they say carefully.

In recent years, the popular Head-to-Head Haiku Competition at the National Poetry Slam has helped bring the haiku into the performance poetry world.

An example of haiku is "Pain Suite" by 2007 Head-to-Head Haiku National Champion Charles Ellik. A suite is a series of haiku that address the same topic.

Reading Questions:

1. *Explain the characteristics of a haiku.*

2. *Pass out copies or put "Pain Suite" on the overhead projector.*

3. *Read the first haiku out loud and ask the students to count the syllables to themselves as you read.*

4. *Ask students if this fits the definition of a haiku. (Yes, it has three lines, the correct amount of syllables, and is nature-themed.)*

5. *Have students break into pairs and read the rest of the haiku. As they read, make sure that they are keeping track of syllables and making sure the haiku adhere to the definition.*

6. *Challenge your students to think more critically about the poems with questioning. In your opinion do the haiku work better individually or as a group? What is the theme that links these poems together? What image appears in your mind as you read these? Which haiku do you think provides the most vivid imagery?*

Writing Prompt:

Challenge them to write their own. As a class, create a list of seemingly basic tasks (brushing your teeth, eating lunch, riding the bus, sitting in homeroom, etc.). Have students pick a task from that list and write their haiku about it. If they are having a hard time deciding what to write about, have a number of tasks already written on slips of paper and have students draw out of a hat or bucket to write about.

"ZOMBIE VEGETARIAN" BY SHAPPY SEASHOLTZ

Persona Poem

A persona poem is a poem written from the first person perspective of someone other than the poet. Basically, the poet puts themselves into another character's shoes. This could be someone from down the block, a television personality, or even an animal or an inanimate object. The poet uses the voice of the character, talks like the character, and reacts like the character. It frees the poet to say things and express thoughts that they would not otherwise say.

An example of this would be "Zombie Vegetarian" by Shappy Seasholtz. Shappy is not a zombie, but he has adopted the language and speaking patterns of a zombie. The impact is most evident when the poem is read aloud.

Reading Questions:

1. *Explain the characteristics of a persona poem.*

2. *Build background knowledge by asking students what they know about zombies and collect their ideas on a board or overhead.*

3. *Tell the students that they are going to read a poem from the perspective of a zombie. Tell them that it is called "Zombie Vegetarian" and have them make predictions about what the poem will be about. What might a zombie vegetarian want to express?*

4. *Pass out copies or put "Zombie Vegetarian" on an overhead projector. Have students read the poem aloud. Encourage them to recite it like a zombie.*

5. *Ask students "What makes this a persona poem?" and have them work in pairs to identify parts of the poem that fit with the definition you provided (first person perspective, dialect, character says "me" instead of "I", brain eating, etc.).*

6. *Have students share and collect the responses.*

7. *Now that they have found the examples, encourage them to think more critically about the poem with questioning: Why would a poet decide to write a poem from this perspective? How would the poem be different if the perspective was changed? How is a zombie vegetarian an example of irony?*

Writing Prompts:

1. *After students share, inform them that they will now be writing their own persona poems. Have students pick a person or thing that they would like to use. Before writing their poems, have the students collect words and ideas that are associated with their character.*

2. Find out who they've been learning about in their history class. Create a list of those people and have students pick one to use as the subject of a persona poem.

Other Persona Poem Examples:

"Mother to Son" by Langston Hughes, "Here in Harlem" by Walter Dean Myers, "Medusa" by Patricia Smith

"SHAKESPEARIAN SONNET FOR E-40" BY JASON BAYANI

Sonnet

Jason Bayani makes an unlikely combination in this poem. He expresses his feelings about E-40 (a Bay Area rapper closely associated with the "Hyphy" scene) by using a Shakespearian sonnet. This lesson would be best used if attached to a Shakespeare or sonnet unit. We recommend using the "Preparing for Sonnets" guide that is in the back of this book before using this poem or any other sonnet.

Pre-Reading Questions:

1. *Ask students what they know about language in different situations: at work, at home, with friends.*

2. *Does the language or dialect differ?*

3. *What would people think of them when they use each of the different language codes?*

4. *Is that fair?*

After Reading Questions:

1. *First ask students to identify words they don't understand. Go over them.*

2. *Then have students identify lines that hit home or stick out.*

3. *How does Bayani use a canon form to discuss racism and classism of modern language?*

4. *Why does the form help to address social expectation and rebel against present politics?*

Writing Prompt:

Again, refer back to "Preparing for Sonnets." Have students complete their own "Frankensonnet."

"WILLIAM SHAKESPEARE GETS HOOKED ON 8-BIT NINTENDO" BY JEREMY RICHARDS

In the Style of...

Writing a poem in the style of a famous poet, or your favorite poet, sounds easy enough, but without an example, the student often struggles. Jeremy Richards is a master of this method. He has taken this method all the way to the Finals stage of the National Poetry Slam. He has written poems in the style of T.S. Eliot, Sylvia Plath, and now William Shakespeare.

It is important to note that Jeremy Richards is not simply copying the poet's style. Instead, he is creating poetry that combines the old master's style with his own modern twist, such as having T.S. Eliot write a gangster rap, or having Shakespeare write about Nintendo.

Questions

1. *How has the poet adopted Shakespeare's style?*
   He has used the dialect of Shakespeare. He uses words like "thy," "thou," and "whilst." These words are not used too often in modern times. Much like Shakespeare would end a sonnet with a rhyming couplet, Jeremy Richards does the same at the end of this poem.

2. *What effect do you think the poet was trying to achieve by combining Shakespeare with Nintendo?*
   He is possibly trying to achieve a comedic effect. Shakespeare is often thought of as serious, and to have him write about Nintendo would be uncharacteristic of him.

3. *Based on what you already know about Shakespeare, do you think this is an accurate portrayal of how he would view Nintendo?*
   Student answers will vary.

Writing Prompt:

Now tell students it's their turn. They have to write a poem in the style of another poet. You can assign them a poet but it would be best to have them choose. It will help to provide a list of poets and poems you've previously studied to help them with their choices.

Name: _____   Date: _____

Questions

1. *How has the poet adopted Shakespeare's style?*

   _____

   _____

   _____

2. *What effect do you think the poet was trying to achieve by combining Shakespeare with Nintendo?*

   _____

   _____

   _____

3. *Based on what you already know about Shakespeare, do you think this is an accurate portrayal of how he would view Nintendo?*

   _____

   _____

   _____

Writing Prompt

Now it's your turn. Write a poem in the style of another poet. Think of writers that you've already learned about. Think of writers who have distinct styles. Pick a poet and write a poem in their style.

"THE FOAM" BY ROBBIE Q TELFER

Visualization

In his poem "The Foam," Robbie Q Telfer uses descriptive language to help the reader create a mental picture of monster known only as "the foam." He also makes allusions to 1950's science fiction movies that could help create the image.

Reading Questions:

1. *Why is the foam so dangerous?*
   The foam is dangerous because it is relentless. It never stops. It also cannot be stopped because it is never hurt.

2. *What is an example of the foam being unstoppable?*
   In the first stanza the foam seeps through the floorboards. If it can get through the tiniest of spaces, there is no way to keep it out. It has also been stabbed and shot, but it only consumes the bullets and grows larger.

3. *How does the third stanza help create an image of the foam?*
   The movie poster is reminiscent of a 1950's science fiction movie like "The Blob." Those posters had huge, menacing looking monsters that were larger than life. You can almost see the foam looming over the motorcycle and the couple just before it swallows them all up.

4. *Why do you think the foam decided to spare the little boy who put the foam on his face?*
   Maybe the foam has a weakness after all. It is possible that the boy was so innocent that the foam decided not hurt him. Everyone else was trying to hurt the foam, but this little boy only wants to play with the foam.

Writing Prompt:

Have students create a movie poster for "The Foam." Show them examples of 50's science fiction posters online and have them use those examples as well as the description in stanza three to create their own poster.

WORKSHEET: "THE FOAM" BY ROBBIE Q TELFER

Name: _____   Date: _____

Reading Questions:

1. *Why is the foam so dangerous?*

    _____

    _____

    _____

2. *What is an example of the foam being unstoppable?*

    _____

    _____

    _____

3. *How does the third stanza help create an image of the foam?*

    _____

    _____

    _____

4. *Why do you think the foam decided to spare the little boy who put the foam on his face?*

    _____

    _____

    _____

Writing Prompt:

Create your own movie poster for "The Foam." Look for sensory details and vivid descriptions to create your own 50's style science fiction poster.

"ZIP-LINES" BY TIM STAFFORD

Utopia/alliteration

Tim Stafford has created an environmental Utopian city in his poem "Zip-Lines." This is a city where the citizens choose to fling themselves across town by cable rather than using subways or automobiles. You can tie this poem into a lesson about alternative power sources, global warming, and green alternatives. Look for alliteration throughout this poem.

Pre-Reading Questions:

1. *What is a Utopia?*
   A utopia is an imagined perfect place or state.

2. *Is a Utopia possible in today's society?*
   Student answers will vary.

After Reading Questions:

1. *How can this zip-line city be classified as a Utopia?*
   The zip-lines have solved a lot of problems. There are no cars so there is no smog. Even the subway conductors were able to find new jobs even though the subway was shut down. Nothing goes to waste and it seems like other cities are trying to mimic their success.

2. *Do you see any ways that the zip-lines would have a negative effect?*
   People might be afraid of heights. There is no mention of weather so what happens if it is raining, snowing, or extremely windy? Zip-lines are small so what would you do if you had to move?

3. *Would your city be better off with a zip-line transit system? Why or why not?*
   Student answers will vary depending on geography.

Writing Prompt:

You have just moved to a zip-line city. What are the good things? What are the bad things? Create a poem or story that describes your daily routines as you move about your new city.

WORKSHEET: "ZIP-LINES" BY TIM STAFFORD

Name: _____   Date: _____

Questions

1. *How can this zip-line city be classified as a Utopia?*

   _____

   _____

   _____

   _____

2. *Do you see any ways that the zip-lines would have a negative effect?*

   _____

   _____

   _____

   _____

3. *Would your city be better off with a zip-line transit system? Why or why not?*

   _____

   _____

   _____

   _____

Writing Prompt:

You have just moved to a zip-line city. What are the good things? What are the bad things? Create a poem or story that describes your daily routines as you move about your new city.

"POWER OUT" BY SHIRA ERLICHMAN

Massachusetts-based poet Shira Erlichman is speaking to someone directly in her poem "Power Out." We don't know who the speaker is. Use the following questions to help students dig deeper into this poem.

Pre-Reading Question:

How does technology positively and negatively affect our ability to communicate?

After Reading Questions:

1. What do you notice about repetition in this poem?

2. What effect does it have on your understanding of the poem? Why?

3. What images stand out? Why?

4. Who is the speaker? How do you know?

5. What is the speaker trying to say?

6. Why does it matter that the TV is gone?

7. How does television affect this poem: what the speaker says, how the speaker communicates, the odd flux of images?

Additional Reading:

"Dover Beach" by Matthew Arnold or "There Will Come Soft Rains" by Sara Teasdale

"PROMISES" BY MOZART GUERREIR

Mozart makes the most out of a little. In this poem he makes comparisons by using simile. Try to see if your students can recognize the simile and then use these questions to find out the reasons behind those comparisons.

Pre Reading Question:

1. *Have you ever made a promise you knew you couldn't keep? What was it?*

After Reading Questions:

1. *Besides the way the poet describes, how are promises and Christmas wrapping paper alike?*
   They both come with a sense of expectation. They make you believe that something good is going to happen. If you are handed a wrapped present and find nothing underneath, you feel let down. This is the same way you feel if someone makes you a promise only to go back on it later.

2. *Why does the poet compare trust to a "dream/in a kinky collar"?*
   The poet wants to trust people but for some reason he cannot. Maybe it's because of all the broken promises. He does offer hope. The dream can be loosened and allowed to get some air so maybe he can lower his guard and begin to trust people.

3. *Can something "be pretty in an ugly kind of way"?*
   Student answers will vary.

Writing Prompt:

Write a poem that explains to someone in the past why you broke a promise to them. Address that person directly in the poem. And, no, you don't have to give it to that person, unless the person you broke a promise to is yourself.

WORKSHEET: "PROMISES" BY MOZART GUERREIR

Name: _____   Date: _____

1. *Have you ever made a promise you knew you couldn't keep? What was it?*

   _____

   _____

   _____

2. *Besides the way the poet describes, how are promises and Christmas wrapping paper alike?*

   _____

   _____

   _____

3. *Why does the poet compare trust to a "dream/in a kinky collar"?*

   _____

   _____

   _____

4. *Can something "be pretty in an ugly kind of way"?*

   _____

   _____

   _____

Writing Prompt:

Write a poem that explains to someone in the past why you broke a promise to them. Address that person directly in the poem. And, no, you don't have to give it to that person, unless the person you broke a promise to is yourself.

"LOVE SONG FOR THE PLASTIC BAG" BY KAREN FINNEYFROCK

Personification

Personification is when a poet gives human attributes to a non-human object or animal. This technique is commonly used in fables.

"Love Song for a Plastic Bag" by Karen Finneyfrock is an excellent example of this technique. The poet has taken an everyday item and through personification has given that object life.

Reading Questions:

1. *Describe personification to your students. Be sure to explain the differences between personification and persona.*

2. *Build background by asking students to recall stories or poems they've read before that use personification. If they can't think of any, mention a fable such as "The Tortoise and the Hare" and have them describe what happened.*

3. *Ask students how they would use personification to describe an object such as a plastic bag.*

4. *Now pass out copies of "Love Song for the Plastic Bag" by Karen Finneyfrock.*

5. *Instruct students that they are going to read the poem and seek out examples of personification. You can have students highlight, underline, or mark with sticky notes. This can be done as a whole class, in small groups, or independently.*

6. *After they have had sufficient time to read, reread, and take notes, begin to gather examples on the board (the bag talks, the bag is born, it cradles, it dangles it feet, etc.).*

7. *Now that they have found the examples, encourage them to think more critically about the poem with questioning: What impact does personification have on this poem? Why do you think the poet decided to use this technique? How does the poet feel about the plastic bag?*

Writing Prompt:

The best way to learn a technique is to practice that technique. Have students pick an everyday object such as a desk, table, chair, or door and have them write a poem about that object that uses personification. If your students are shy, have some objects written on slips of paper and have them pull one at random and have them write about whatever is on their slip.

Other Examples of Personification:

"April Rain Song" by Langston Hughes, "Once by the Pacific" by Robert Frost

"BENEDICTION FOR PROM NIGHT" BY CRISTIN O'KEEFE APTOWICZ

List Poem

A list poem is one of the most popular poetic forms, especially with beginning poets. The form is flexible and encourages the poet to draw from their own personal experiences. But poet be warned! It is easy for a list poem to become boring. The list should be skillfully put together to get the desired effect. "Benediction for Prom Night" by Cristin O'Keefe Aptowicz is an example of an engaging list poem. (Be sure to explain that a benediction is the saying of a blessing.)

Pre-Reading Question:

Why do we put more importance on some events in our life and less on others?

After Reading Questions:

1. *Why do you think the poet chose to write this poem about a prom night instead of another event in her life?*
   Proms are ritualistic. Different areas put their own twists on it, but basically a prom is a prom. Since it is a ritual or rite of passage, it makes sense that she uses a benediction to bless the event.

2. *Do you think the poet is writing from personal experience, or is she making it all up?*
   Student answers will vary, but make sure they notice the use of specific details.

3. *Why do you think the poet chose to break up the poem into three different lists as opposed to one big list?*
   The stanzas go in order of the event. When someone is going to a prom they must first deal with the agony of getting ready as described in the first stanza. Then they have to worry about things that could go wrong at the event itself as is described in the second stanza. Then, after sorting out all the details, they get to enjoy the moment as described in the third stanza.

4. *Why do you think the poet chose this form for this topic?*
   She chose this form possibly to emphasize all the work and worry that goes into a single night, and also to show how the simple joy of a slow dance can make all the drama seem ridiculous. It also adds elements of humor to the poem.

Writing Prompt

Pick an important event in your life. This could be graduation, basketball game, track meet, first date, mid-terms, etc. Create a list poem about that day that gives the reader a sense of what it would be like to participate in that event. Use vivid sensory details in your list poem to make it come alive.

WORKSHEET: "BENEDICTION FOR PROM NIGHT" BY CRISTIN O'KEEFE APTOWICZ

Name: _____   Date: _____

Questions:

1. *Why do you think the poet chose to write this poem about a prom night instead of another event in her life?*

   _____

   _____

   _____

2. *Do you think the poet is writing from personal experience, or is she making it all up?*

   _____

   _____

   _____

3. *Why do you think the poet chose to break up the poem into three different lists as opposed to one big list?*

   _____

   _____

   _____

4. *Why do you think the poet chose this form for this topic?*

   _____

   _____

   _____

Writing Prompt

Pick an important event in your life. This could be graduation, basketball game, track meet, first date, mid-terms, etc. Create a list poem about that day that gives the reader a sense of what it would be like to participate in that event. Use vivid sensory details in your list poem to make it come alive.

"CLOCKWORK" BY KEITH MORRIS KURZMAN

Pattern

Pattern refers to the way a poet organizes their poem. They do this by combining rhyme schemes, stanza, and meter into an organized piece. In "Clockwork" by Keith Morris Kurzman, you can see a definite pattern that is set up by stanzas and repetition.

Pre-Reading Question:

Why do people put their dreams on hold?

After Reading Questions:

1. *What are the patterns in this poem?*
   The pattern is the repetition of numbered stanzas that refer to age in between larger, unnumbered stanzas. The large stanzas begin and end with the same lines.

2. *Why do you think the poet begins the larger stanzas with, "Still—every night you dream about. . . ."?*
   The numbered stanzas list milestones that come with age. As the person gets older, the milestones become more and more mundane. By starting off with the same line it shows that no matter how caught up people get, they can still dream and hope to possibly break the cycle.

3. *Why do you think the poet ends with the line, "but not today, not today because the Clockwork is ticking. . . ."?*
   This shows that even though people know what they need to do, it is easy to put things off. Unfortunately, every day that it is postponed is a day lost and it only becomes harder to break the cycle.

4. *What does "The Clockwork" represent?*
   "The Clockwork" is a metaphor for life. No one can live forever. No matter how much we do or how hard we try, our time is finite. Therefore we need to quit dreaming and begin doing. If not, you will be stuck in a formulaic existence.

WORKSHEET: "CLOCKWORK" BY KEITH MORRIS KURZMAN

Name: _____   Date: _____

Questions:

1. *What are the patterns in this poem?*

_____

_____

_____

_____

2. *Why do you think the poet begins the larger stanzas with, "Still—every night you dream about. ..."?*

_____

_____

_____

_____

3. *Why do you think the poet ends with the line, "but not today, not today because the Clockwork is ticking. . . ."?*

_____

_____

_____

_____

4. *What does "The Clockwork" represent?*

_____

_____

_____

_____

"FOR THOSE WHO CAN STILL RIDE AN AIRPLANE FOR THE FIRST TIME" BY ANIS MOJGANI

Simile

A simile is a comparison between two unlike objects that uses the words "like" or "as." It's a poetic device that adds layers and depth to poem. The former World Slam Champion Anis Mojgani uses this technique in much of his poetry.

Pre-Reading Questions:

1. *Explain what a simile is.*

2. *Try to have students think of ones they have heard before: "dumb as an ox," "big as a house," "chews like a cow," "party like a rock star," etc.*

3. *Have them explain what the comparison means.*

4. *Tell them they will be reading a poem that uses simile as a poetic device and their job is to read through and underline the lines that contain the simile.*

5. *Collect the similes on the board.*

6. *Ask them to try to explain what the simile means.*

After Reading Questions:

1. *What does the poet mean when he says, "My fingers they open up like gates when I type"?*
   When a gate opens, it allows you to enter a private or guarded area. Maybe the poet means that when he writes, it's his way of allowing the reader to take a peek into his personal affairs.

2. *Why does he say Quentin's fingers are "little like the stems of flowers"?*
   To show the reader that Quentin is small and delicate. He is beautiful like a flower and just as fragile.

3. *What does the poet mean when he says, "watching a small boy float down like fresh water"?*
   By comparing the boy to fresh water, you get the sense that this boy is pure and innocent. He is young enough to not be polluted by other people's feelings and opinions. He is genuine and able to do as he pleases without worrying about what others think. If something is in his way he simply flows around it like the water.

Additional Reading for Simile:

"A Dream Deferred" by Langston Hughes, "Like" by Mike McGee

Name: _____   Date: _____

Questions:

1. *What does the poet mean when he says, "My fingers they open up like gates when I type"?*

    _____

    _____

    _____

    _____

2. *Why does he say Quentin's fingers are "little like the stems of flowers"?*

    _____

    _____

    _____

    _____

3. *What does the poet mean when he says, "watching a small boy float down like fresh water"?*

    _____

    _____

    _____

    _____

Writing Prompt

Anis talks about growing up and some of the things that have changed since he was a kid. Write a poem that tells the reader what you were like when you were younger. Use at least three similes to describe yourself.

"WHY GRAMMA GROWS OLD WITH G.I. JOE" BY DEJA TAYLOR

Imagery

When you read a story or a poem, you begin to create a picture in your mind. Although there are no illustrations or photographs in the book, you could describe what the characters or the setting looks like. This is because the author has used imagery. Imagery is when the author uses words that appeal to the senses to create an image in the reader's mind. Former Louder Than a Bomb finalist and hip hop artist Deja Taylor uses imagery to put the reader in her Gramma Peggy's house.

After Reading Questions:

1. *In the first stanza, the poet says, "Gramma Peggy's house/is older than she is." What descriptive details does she use to create an image of this old house?*
   She says that the dust is the only thing keeping it together. Therefore it must be somewhat dilapidated. It might be a house that creaks and cracks. The packed dust also implies that it must be in a state of neglect, maybe because her Gramma's boys have all gone and she has no one to help.

2. *What details does she use to create the image of the "my stuff" box?*
   The box is probably from when her uncle was very young because the words are just scribbled across the top. It had been sitting untouched for a while because so much dust had collected that it hid the orange color of the box. When she wiped it, it must have left streaks of bright color on the box and a thick coating of dust on her fingertips.

3. *How does the poet compare the G.I. Joe figure to her uncles?*
   The G.I. Joe figure has begun to deteriorate with time. The paint is fading, and it looks like he is balding. Her uncles are deteriorating with age as well. Only they don't live in a plastic box, they live in apartments, or "boxes they pay rent in." G.I. Joe fought imaginary wars while her uncles are "the kind who fight through life."

4. *Why do you think the poet made that comparison?*
   Student answers will vary.

Writing Prompt:

Make a short list of people you associate with your childhood or a moment of growing up (school, a grandmother's house, etc.). When you pick a person as a focus, choose a location that's associated with the person and an object that can be found there. Create a sense of space focusing on sensory details (smell, taste, touch, sound, and sight). Take the reader on a tour of a place that you spent a lot of time in as a child. Make sure that you clearly describe it.

WORKSHEET: "WHY GRAMMA GROWS OLD WITH G.I. JOE" BY DEJA TAYLOR

Name: _____   Date: _____

Reading Questions:

1. *In the first stanza, the poet says, "Gramma Peggy's house/is older than she is." What descriptive details does she use to create an image of this old house?*

_____

_____

_____

2. *What details does she use to create the image of the "my stuff" box?*

_____

_____

_____

3. *How does the poet compare the G.I. Joe figure to her uncles?*

_____

_____

_____

4. *Why do you think the poet made that comparison?*

_____

_____

_____

Writing Prompt:

Make a short list of people you associate with your childhood or a moment of growing up (school, a grandmother's house, etc.). When you pick a person as a focus, choose a location that's associated with the person and an object that can be found there. Create a sense of space focusing on sensory details (smell, taste, touch, sound, sight). Take the reader on a tour of a place that you spent a lot of time in as a child. Make sure that you clearly describe it.

"OLD SENRYU" BY BEN BUTTER

Senryu

At first glance a senryu looks a lot like a haiku. They are very similar in many ways, but there some important differences. The main difference is that a senryu is meant to be funny. It is the original method of "playing the dozens." Poets would get together and add a stanza on top of another stanza trying to outdo each other as they went along.

Senryu also do not necessarily follow the 5-7-5 syllable structure as haiku. Some do, but the senryu is the less formal cousin of the haiku.

An example of a senryu is "Old Senryu" by Ben Butter.

Reading Questions:

1. *Explain the characteristics of a senryu. Be sure to explain the difference between senryu and haiku.*

2. *Pass out copies or put "Several Old Senryu" on the overhead projector.*

3. *Read aloud, or have one student per senryu read.*

4. *Put students into small groups and assign each group a different senryu.*

5. *Ask them to answer the following questions: What is the poet making fun of? What evidence in the poem can you use to back up your answer? Can you give an example from your life that is similar to what is being said in the poem?*

6. *Answers will vary from poem to poem and class to class, but be sure to have a volunteer from each group give at least one example.*

7. *After discussing interpretations and examples, have students remain in their groups.*

Writing Prompts:

Have them pick one topic for the group or assign topics for each group to write their own senryu about. A suggested topic is the teacher. Have students write senryu that make fun of the teacher. It is a win-win for everybody. The students get to blow off a little steam at the teacher's expense, and the teacher gets their students writing and utilizing a new poetic form.

"YOU MAKE HOLY WAR" BY AJA MONET

Make sure your students know what a holy war is before reading this poem. Compare a holy war to another type of war like Vietnam or WWII. Let your students know what they have in common and how they differ.

Pre-Reading Questions:

1. In what ways are relationships positive? Negative?

2. In what ways does a relationship cause an inner conflict?

3. How do relationships change people (for better or worse)?

After Reading Questions:

1. What lines do students like? Why do they like them?

2. What images pertain to war?

3. Why does Monet choose to title the poem "You Make Holy War" instead of "You Make War"? What's the difference?

Writing Prompts:

What does man or woman think of your creation? What does God/the universe think of you?

or

Write a poem of praise for someone or a relationship using a negative, difficult, or highly political comparison (holy war, revolution, human sacrifice).

WORKSHEET: "YOU MAKE HOLY WAR" BY AJA MONET

Name: _____   Date: _____

Questions:

1. What lines do you like best? Why do you like them?

_____

_____

_____

2. What images pertain to war?

_____

_____

_____

3. Why does Monet choose to title the poem "You Make Holy War" instead of "You Make War"? What's the difference?

_____

_____

_____

Writing Prompt (pick one):

What does man or woman think of your creation? What does God/the universe think of you?

or

Write a poem of praise for someone or a relationship using a negative, difficult, or highly political comparison (holy war, revolution, human sacrifice).

"HECTOR LAVOE IS GOD" BY CARLOS ANDRES GOMEZ

Layout

Why do most poems have their lines aligned on the left side of the page? Will it look ridiculous if it is done differently? Poets have been using abstract methods to display poetry for centuries. Poets like George Herbert and Apollinaire were famous for writing calligrams, or shaped poetry. Although not as abstract as a calligram, the NYC poet and actor Carlos Andres Gomez has taken an unconventional approach to the layout of his poem "Hector Lavoe is God."

Questions:

1. *How does the layout of this poem differ from that of most poems in this book?*
   The other poems are all aligned left while this poem is centered.

2. *What impact does this layout have on you as a reader?*
   Since it is the only poem with this layout, it pops out from the rest. Even before reading a word, the reader is drawn into it. It offers something more visual than the other poems.

3. *Why do you think the poet chose this layout for this poem?*
   The whole poem is about dancing. He uses a lot of language that deals with movement like pulsing, writhing, burst, contorting, etc. If you look at the poem, it looks like it is pulsing with the rhythm of the music. It helps build up to the end of the poem.

4. *Do you think the poem would have more or less of an impact if it had a more traditional left-aligned layout?*
   Student answers will vary.

Writing Prompt:
Think of an action. Think of the movements that go along with that action. Arrange the text on the page to create a poem whose form reflects that action.

WORKSHEET: "HECTOR LAVOE IS GOD" BY CARLOS ANDRES GOMEZ

Name: _____   Date: _____

Questions

1. How does the layout of this poem differ from that of most poems in this book?

_____

_____

_____

2. What impact does this layout have on you as a reader?

_____

_____

_____

3. Why do you think the poet chose this layout for this poem?

_____

_____

_____

4. Do you think the poem would have more or less of an impact if it had a more traditional left-aligned layout?

_____

_____

_____

Writing Prompt:

Think of an action. Think of the movements that go along with that action. Arrange the text on the page to create a poem whose form reflects that action.

"WRITE A POEM ABOUT MONSTERS" BY CRISTIN O'KEEFE APTOWICZ

Writer's Block

This poem talks about the ways in which the poet tries to inspire herself to write. Most of her methods do not work, and she explains why. This is a great poem to use when talking to your students about writer's block.

Pre-Reading Questions:

1. *What is writer's block?*

2. *Can it be prevented? If so, how?*

After Reading Questions:

1. *Why is the speaker having trouble writing about the ideas she has come up with?*
   Some of the ideas simply don't make sense when looked at later. Others just don't interest her. The "Poem about Monsters" is a poem that she really wants to write but she'd afraid of doing it wrong.

2. *Why is it important for her to write the "Poem about Monsters" the "right" way as opposed to the other ideas like Neck Face or twin Sestinas for Twins?*
   The other ideas seem random while "Poem about Monsters" is rooted in experience. She has specific memories that relate to that poem so it's more important to her personally. She doesn't have any connection to the other ideas.

3. *How does the poet use her writer's block to create a poem?*
   She's able to use her writer's block by writing about it. She talks about the challenges, her ideas, and memories. Although it might not be the way she wanted, the reader is still able to see the importance of the monsters.

WORKSHEET: "WRITE A POEM ABOUT MONSTERS" BY CRISTIN O'KEEFE APTOWICZ

Name: _____   Date: _____

Questions:

1. Why is the speaker having trouble writing about the ideas she has come up with?

_____

_____

_____

_____

_____

2. Why is it important for her to write the "Poem about Monsters" the "right" way as opposed to the other ideas like Neck Face or twin Sestinas for Twins?

_____

_____

_____

_____

_____

3. How does the poet use her writer's block to create a poem?

_____

_____

_____

_____

_____

"WRITING PROMPTS 2008" BY IDRIS GOODWIN

In this poem Idris Goodwin commands the reader to "Write." He is no longer content with the reader simply observing; he wants them to participate. To help them along the way, he has included a variety of different things to write about. This simple lesson was inspired by a workshop led by poet/educator Robbie Q Telfer.

1. Hand out a copy of "Writing Prompts 2008" to each student.

2. Read aloud or allow students to read independently.

3. After reading the poem, have the students go back and circle the five commands that they liked the best.

4. Allow students to share one that they picked and ask them why they chose that particular command.

5. After briefly discussing the reasons, tell the students that they have to pick one of the five they chose and write about it.

6. Let them know that they can switch commands if they are having a difficult time but encourage them to stick with their first pick.

7. Allow ten minutes for them to write. If they are still writing at the end of the ten minutes, allow additional time.

8. When the time is up, have students share what they wrote.

9. If time allows, repeat steps 5 thru 9 by having students pick a different command.

"LIFE: (UN)TITLED" BY BONAFIDE ROJAS

Bonafide Rojas has tried editing his life into good verses. He uses punctuation, poetic form, and fonts to symbolize different parts of his life. See if you and your students can figure out what those things symbolize and then have students edit their own lives.

Pre-Reading Question:

If you could edit your life into just the good parts while removing the bad, would you? Why?

After Reading Questions:

1. *How does Bonafide acknowledge his weaknesses in this poem?*
   In the fifth stanza he admits to having a big ego because he compares it to large fonts. He also admits that he's not good at rhyming, he's unsure of his career path, and he wants to keep his life simple but is unable to do so.

2. *Why would he rather live his life as a haiku rather than an epic?*
   An epic is a long, complicated story with many twists and turns. A haiku is short and simple. Both forms have a larger meaning but the haiku is able to strip away the excess and it allows the reader to focus.

3. *Why do you think he wants to be remembered as Steven Rojas instead of Bonafide Rojas?*
   Student answers will vary.

Writing Prompt:

How can you use poetry to represent your life? Write a poem that uses punctuation, poetic forms, and fonts to symbolize different parts of your life. Write about your past but more importantly, write about how you want your future to be represented.

WORKSHEET: "LIFE: (UN)TITLED" BY BONAFIDE ROJAS

Name: _____   Date: _____

Questions:

1. *How does Bonafide acknowledge his weaknesses in this poem?*

   _____

   _____

   _____

   _____

2. *Why would he rather live his life as a haiku rather than an epic?*

   _____

   _____

   _____

   _____

3. *Why do you think he wants to be remembered as Steven Rojas instead of Bonafide Rojas?*

   _____

   _____

   _____

   _____

Writing Prompt:

How can you use poetry to represent your life? Write a poem that uses punctuation, poetic forms, and fonts to symbolize different parts of your life. Write about your past but more importantly, write about how you want your future to be represented.

"AUTOBIOGRAPHY #32" BY DAVID ALLYON

In this poem, David Allyon creates an autobiography that is fictional. He plays on the idea of celebrity and creates an autobiography on that idea. Use this poem to help students write their own autobiographies or to create fake ones for other people.

Reading Questions:

1. *Put on the board, "You have one page to write your autobiography. What do you include?"*

2. *Share the answers and collect them on the board.*

3. *Read the poem as a class and have students look for items from their list.*

4. *Ask "What has the poet included/excluded from your list? Why did he do that?"*

5. *Now bring up the idea of celebrity.*

6. *Ask your students, "How does Ayllon use celebrities' lives as a conceit for his own?"*

7. *"Why would he use the life as a celebrity to represent his own?"*

8. *Introduce the writing prompt.*

Writing Prompt:

Pick a type of person, class, or job to help explain your life (a waitress, princess, street urchin, etc.).

(optional) Begin with "When I was born" or "I was born."

"FISHING FOR SATELLITES" BY CHARLEY POPE

Tall Tale

Charley Pope has created something that is part poem and part tall tale. It is a blend of hyperbole and sincerity. Use this poem as part of a larger unit on tall tales, myths, and folklore.

Pre-Reading Questions:

1. *What is a tall tale?*
   It is a story with unbelievable or exaggerated elements that is told as if it were true. The narrator of the story sometimes puts himself into the tale.

2. *What is its purpose?*
   Some tall tales are used as creation myths, such as Paul Bunyon dragging his ax and creating the Grand Canyon. Some tall tales are used simply as bragging rights. Someone who hears a story about a person eating 60 hot dogs might come back and say they witnessed a man eat 100 hot dogs and still go back for dessert.

After Reading Questions:

1. *In what way does Pope create a tall tale for his father?*
   The poem is entirely exaggerated, but he plays it off as if it actually happened. He takes the story his father told and elaborates even further. It's as if he is trying to top his father's story to prove himself.

2. *How does the story change once he tries to do what his father did?*
   He takes his father's already incredible story and takes it even further. He pulls down more than just satellites, and instead of Sputnik, he pulls down the Hubble telescope. Unlike Sputnik, the Hubble actually speaks to him. He has modernized his father's story.

3. *Who has the most believable story, Charley or his father?*
   Student answers will vary.

Writing Prompt:

Pick a habit or routine for an older family member.

Make it larger than life (instead of catching fish, they catch satellites).

Did you learn how to do it from them? Even if the answer is no, how did it affect you?

WORKSHEET: "FISHING FOR SATELLITES" BY CHARLEY POPE

Name: _____   Date: _____

1. *In what way does Pope create a tall tale for his father?*

    _____

    _____

    _____

    _____

2. *How does the story change once he tries to do what his father did?*

    _____

    _____

    _____

    _____

3. *Who has the most believable story, Charley or his father?*

    _____

    _____

    _____

    _____

Writing Prompt:

Pick a habit or routine for an older family member.

Make it larger than life (instead of catching fish, they catch satellites).

Did you learn how to do it from them? Even if the answer is no, how did it affect you?

"TO THE LIGHTNING TEACHERS" BY DERRICK BROWN

This poem contains some common phrases and clichés. However, the poet has put his own spin on them to give them new meaning. This lesson helps students identify clichés and shows them how to put a fresh spin on the words.

Pre-Reading Questions:

What is a cliché? How do you identify them?

How do you "flip" a cliché?

Note: This is a good time to talk about colloquialism and metaphor. There are two parts of metaphor: the tenor and the vehicle. The tenor is the abstract or object that is being defined. The vehicle drives the comparison home.

My love is a rose.
    | |
  tenor   vehicle

Heard this one? How do you change it? The easiest way to flip a cliché is to change vehicles:

My love is a fresh cup of coffee.

Another way is to extend the comparison so that the saying becomes new:

My love is a rose, clipped from the neighbor's rose garden, sneering from the vase.

After Reading Questions:

What sayings are familiar to you in the poem?

How does Brown flip the clichés to make the saying new?

Writing Prompt:

Make a list of people who have an effect on your life or who have jobs that work with people, and then make a list of five random objects and a list of five objects associated with the person/job.

Pick one from each list.

Include three pieces of advice or commands to help the person in his/her job.

Write a poem of praise/advice.

"COME ALIVE" BY DERRICK BROWN

Derrick Brown invokes the image of Narnia to address his fears about aging. In his poem "Come Alive," he encourages the reader to do anything except act their age.

Pre-reading Questions:

What are habits that get lost as we grow older?

What pastimes becoming out of date in modern times?

After Reading Questions:

1. *Why does the poet use the imaginary city of Narnia as opposed to an actual city like Seattle or Tokyo?*
   He refers to Narnia because it is a fantasy. In order to picture Narnia you must have an imagination, which is something people lose as they get older. Even if they don't lose it, they are less likely to share it with others. By using Narnia, he insists that you crank up your imagination and join him in Narnia.

2. *What is ironic about his declarations as mayor?*
   You traditionally think of a mayor as being a serious person who wields some power. They are in charge of things so they do not have time for trivial pursuits. In this poem, however, he insists that you climb trees, dip your hands in butter, and get young.

3. *How does Brown use this poem as a call to arms for reading?*
   By using personification, he gives life to the trees. They become soldiers in the war for the lands of imagination. If they are willing to sacrifice their lives so that we can read, it makes reading seem like a much nobler pursuit than some seem to realize.

4. *What does the poet mean when he says "you've been away from Narnia for awhile, welcome back"?*
   Student answers will vary.

Writing Prompt

Write a poem to yourself 20 years in the future. What do you want your future self to remember to do in 20 years? Be specific as to why you want them to keep doing those things.

WORKSHEET: "COME ALIVE" BY DERRICK BROWN

Name: _____   Date: _____

Questions:

1. *Why does the poet use the imaginary city of Narnia as opposed to an actual city like Seattle or Tokyo?*

   _____

   _____

   _____

2. *What is ironic about his declarations as mayor?*

   _____

   _____

   _____

3. *How does Brown use this poem as a call to arms for reading?*

   _____

   _____

   _____

4. *What does the poet mean when he says "you've been away from Narnia for awhile, welcome back"?*

   _____

   _____

   _____

Writing Prompt

Write a poem to yourself 20 years in the future. What do you want your future self to remember to do in 20 years? Be specific as to why you want them to keep doing those things.

SUPPLEMENTAL MATERIALS

PANTOUM ORGANIZER

Name: _____   Date: _____

A pantoum is a form developed in Malayan literature. It is a poem made up of four-line stanzas. There is no limit on how many stanzas there can be. The poem contains repeated lines that connect from stanza to stanza. Lines 2 and 4 are taken from one stanza and repeated as lines 1 and 3 in the next.

Poem title: _____

_____Line 1

_____ Line 2

_____ Line 3

_____ Line 4

_____ Line 5- same as line 2

_____ Line 6

_____ Line 7- same as line 4

_____ Line 8

_____ Line 9- same as line 6

_____ Line 10

_____ Line 11-same as line 8

_____ Line 12

SESTINA ORGANIZER

Name: _____   Date: _____

A sestina is a form that is fixed on the number six. There are six stanzas with six unrhymed lines. The words at the end of each line reappear in different order from stanza to stanza. For instance, if I used the word "fix" at the end of line A, I will end every line labeled A with "fix" throughout the entire poem. The poem is completed by a three-line stanza called a tercet that uses all six end words.

Stanza 1

_____ A

_____ B

_____ C

_____ D

_____ E

_____ F

Stanza 2

_____ F

_____ A

_____ E

_____ B

_____ D

_____ C

Stanza 3

_____ C

_____ F

_____ D

_____ A

_____ B

_____ E

Stanza 4

_____E

_____C

_____B

_____F

_____A

_____D

Stanza 5

_____D

_____E

_____A

_____C

_____F

_____B

Stanza 6

_____B

_____D

_____F

_____E

_____C

_____A

Stanza 7 (Tercet)

_____A_____B

_____C_____D

_____E_____F

PREPARING FOR SONNETS

These lessons on sonnets and iambic pentameter take approximately four to five days. You may use all or none. There are handouts included.

Rhythm and Meter:

Start with a list of the rhythms on the board or overhead projector. Use both the word and the illustration of the stress (—) and unstress (U). You do not need to use these particular symbols. These are the ones commonly used because the stress pounds down on the syllable. Come up with ones that work for you.

Go over a word or phrase that demonstrates each rhythm.

Iamb U— (today, before, tonight, again)

Trochee —-U (daisy, autumn, single)

Anapest UU— (of the day, unaware, in the night)

Dactyl —-UU (wonderful, shamelessness, memory)

Amphibrach U—U (remember, October, unable)

Spondee — — is usually used as an extra syllable or an interjection. It is rare (but not impossible) to see a spondaic foot.

Pyrric UU is pretty much impossible. You may find one extra syllable that doesn't receive stress, but you don't find this alone.

After this, ask students to find their name in the rhythm. Most will be trochees.

If time allows, go over Meter.

Poetry walks one foot at a time just like we do. One unit of rhythm (one iamb, one trochee) is called a "foot."

Most of the students will recognize the roots for the meter. Have them guess the name for the number of feet. Each line of a poem contains a certain number of feet of iambs, trochees, spondees, dactyls, or anapests. A line of one foot is a monometer, two feet is a dimeter, and so on—trimeter (three), tetrameter (four), pentameter (five), hexameter (six), heptameter (seven), and octameter (eight). Of course the number of syllables in a line varies according to the rhythm.

Depending on where you stop, please review and move forward before going over the next activity.

Rhythm and Meter

The next activity is a kinesthetic exercise for your students. Have your students stand in a circle, oval, or square. Read line five. After reading, stomp it out. Students must alternate feet for each syllable. Then read and stomp together. Then just stomp. They may need a couple of tries to feel the rhythm. Then ask them if they notice a pattern. Have them count syllables if they need help with meter. Stomping out free verse is always silly. It helps get them up. You may also have them clap the rhythm. You may use this list to compare prose and free verse and to compare rhythms. See notes (rhythm, meter, author). You may also make your own list for them depending on what they need. Using a lot of Shakespeare will help transition from poetry to Shakespeare.

Rhythm and Meter—Teacher Version

1. *And dropped my eyes, unwilling to explain—Iambic Pentameter—Frost*

2. *Double, Double toil and trouble—Trochaic Tetrameter—Shakespeare*

3. *This shoe is my father. No, this left shoe is my father; no, no, this left shoe is my mother—Prose—Shakespeare*

4. *I'll charm the air to give a sound—Iambic Tetrameter—Shakespeare*

5. *So foul and fair a day I have not seen—Iambic Pentameter—Shakespeare*

6. *What once made us weak in the knees ends up just making us weak—Free Verse—Mary Fons*

7. *Think but this and all is mended—Trochaic Tetrameter—Shakespeare*

8. *My mistress' eyes are nothing like the sun—Iambic Pentameter—Shakespeare*

9. *that would mean when the old one died she would be less/dependent on her spirit so/she said—Free Verse—Giovanni*

10. *Oh mother, mother where is happiness?—Iambic Pentameter—Brooks*

Iambic Pentameter

Talk about how to write lines of iambic pentameter.

Start with a banal line: I walked to Mom's and drank a quart of milk.

Then pick a monosyllabic word for the end of a line, and see if the class can help you write a line of iambic pentameter.

Print out some rhyming words. You may use those provided or make your own. Online rhyming dictionaries make this easy. Give each student two or three rhyming words. Their homework is to write two to three lines of perfect iambic pentameter that ENDS with the word(s) you gave them. Try to arrange it so there are four of each rhyme. Their line should rhyme with someone else's. If there's time, let them try it in class. Encourage them to clap or stomp it out.

Sonnets

Use these sonnets to help go over form:

"The Sonnet Ballad" by Gwendolyn Brooks,

"If I should learn, in some quite casual way" by Edna St. Vincent Millay,

"Sonnet 19 (When I consider how my light is spent)" by John Milton,

and "Sonnet 18 (Shall I compare thee to a summer's day)" by William Shakespeare.

You may give a mini-lecture on rhyme scheme and form (quatrains, couplets, octave, sestet, etc.). The next activity becomes a test for notes.

The final test is the Frankensonnet. Students bring in one line on a slip of paper. You may have slips present with markers. Make sure students sign them. Give them 15-20 minutes to make at least two (three or four depending on class size) silly sonnets with perfect rhythm, meter, and rhyme. Offer points or extra credit. Go through and check as they think they're done. You may tape them together and put them up or use a large post-it. Collect all slips for a homework grade.

RHYTHM AND METER

1. *And dropped my eyes, unwilling to explain.*

2. *Double, Double toil and trouble.*

3. *This shoe is my father. No, this left shoe is my father; no, no, this left shoe is my mother.*

4. *I'll charm the air to give a sound.*

5. *So foul and fair a day I have not seen.*

6. *What once made us weak in the knees ends up just making us weak.*

7. *Think but this and all is mended.*

8. *My mistress' eyes are nothing like the sun.*

9. *that would mean when the old one died she would be less/dependent on her spirit so/she said.*

10. *Oh mother, mother where is happiness?*

RHYMING WORDS

scar	right	born
star	light	scorn
car	fight	worn
far	go	torn
day	glow	learn
stay	flow	burn
say	throw	earn
clay	show	turn
way	low	stern
gray	neat	you
stray	heat	blue
play	seat	clue
night	treat	shore
bright	eat	four
sight	tweet	store

POETRY REPORT

Name: _____   Date: _____

Begin by copying your poem on the back of this sheet. Don't photocopy it; write it out.

Name of Poem: _____

Name of Poet: _____

Book Title & Page Number: _____

Read over the poem several times as you answer these questions:

1. *What images (sights, sounds, smells, touches, tastes) do you get from the poem?*

2. *Does it rhyme?*

3. *What examples of repetition do you find? Remember: sounds, words, and/or phrases can be repeated.*

4. *Who is the speaker (age, sex, occupation, attitude) of this poem? Quote a line or two that tells you about the speaker. What does he/she/it seem to value? Who is the speaker talking to?*

5. *What general ideas does the poem seem to be about? What lines show those ideas best? Copy two or more lines here.*

6. *What made you choose this poem? (Do not say "I liked it.") What is about the poem that you like—the sounds, topic, images, etc.?*

SUPPLEMENTAL PERFORMANCE MATERIALS

WHAT IS A POETRY SLAM?

A poetry slam is a poetry competition. Unlike an open mic, there is a winner. Poets are scored by judges usually picked at random from the audience. It was created by former construction worker Marc (So What!) Smith at the Green Mill Jazz Club in Chicago, Illinois as a way to bring the audience into the performance. More than that, it put the audience in control. For a detailed and colorful history, check out the book *Spoken Word Revolution* by Marc Smith and Mark Eleveld.

Should I do a Poetry Slam with my students?

Eventually, yes. Some people are terrified of reading their poems out loud. The thought of having them scored is even worse. Start off with an open mic to get students used to reading their poems out loud in front of an audience. Give them performance suggestions to help build confidence. For the students who already have performance skills or are progressing quicker, do a small slam with those students. Make it an open invitation so that students who are still building up to their level can try it out when they feel they are ready.

Remember: The purpose of a poetry slam is not to have a winner and a loser but to make reading poetry more fun.

Where should I stage a slam?

All you really need is a space. The scale is up to you.

Classroom—You can do a slam in your classroom with little preparation. Arrange the seats so they are focused on the poet. You can put up a music stand or podium so they have something to set their papers on. You won't need a microphone.

Gym/theatre—Use whatever space that your school uses for assembly. The bigger the space, the bigger the audience. Make sure your students have had a lot of experience speaking in front of a crowd before you have them read at such a large venue. It would also help if you've showed them how to adjust and speak into a microphone beforehand.

Outside—Is the sun shining? Then go out to the park, courtyard, lawn, etc. and stage your poetry slam there.

HOW DO I STAGE A POETRY SLAM?

Here are the basic rules of a poetry slam:

Time Limit—Every poet has three minutes to read their poem. If they go over three minutes, they have a ten-second grace period. If they go over 3:10, they lose .5 points per ten seconds.

Judges—Judges score the poet on a scale of 1–10, 1 being the lowest score and 10 being perfect. They can use decimal points but encourage them to only use one decimal point.

Original Work—The poet has to read their own work in a poetry slam.

No Props—Poets cannot use any props in their performance. They can read their poem off of paper but no other objects can be brought onstage.

Those are the basics but you can manipulate those rules if you want. For instance, the number of judges you have is up to you, though it is recommended that you use an odd number. Do whatever fits your situation.

Procedure

1. Once you have the poets signed in, put their names in a hat or have them draw numbers to determine the order. Keep it random to be as fair as possible. The number of poets who participate is entirely up to you.

2. Write down the order and make sure they know who they follow in the poetry slam.

3. Pick judges. If possible, try to use judges that are not students. A lot of middle schools and high schools use teachers, administrators, cafeteria staff, security guards, etc.

4. Read the rules of the slam to the audience. This lets the audience in on the competition and builds tension.

5. Introduce the judges to the audience.

6. Bring up the Calibration Poet. The Calibration Poet is someone who is not part of the actual competition. Their job is to set the stage and let the judges set their bar.

7. Introduce the first poet and encourage the audience to applause.

8. After they have performed, get the scores from the judges. You can do this publicly or privately. You can announce the scores as you go or wait until the end.

9. Go through the rest of the poets until everyone has read and repeat steps 7 and 8.

10. Second Round. It is up to you if you want to do a second or third round. Usually the top 3 or 4 poets are allowed to read another poem in the second round.

11. Announce the winner!

Again, there is flexibility in a poetry slam. You get to pick the number of poets, judges, and rounds. Some slams are more specific in their rules. The Chicago Teen Slam "Louder than a Bomb" stipulates that you cannot use any racist, homophobic, or sexist language. In the end you have to do what fits your students and your school.

POETRY SLAM VARIATIONS

For almost as long as there has been a poetry slam, there have been people putting their own twist on it. See if any of these would work in your classroom.

Head-to-Head Haiku—This is an annual event at the National Poetry Slam. Poets compete against each other but they can only use haiku.

Limerick Slam—Similar to Head-to-Head Haiku only with limericks instead of haiku.

(Insert Poetic Form Here) Slam—Are you studying Shakespeare? Have a Sonnet Slam! You can use any poetic form and have a slam with it. Pantoums, sestinas, odes, whatever you've been working on.

Prop Slam—Props are usually illegal, but in this competition the only thing illegal is NOT using a prop, like a stuffed animal or a light saber. Make sure it relates to the poem.

Cover Slam–This slam throws out the rule of performing only original work. Poets get to pick their favorite poems and perform them. Got a poem by Robert Frost that you have memorized? This is the time to use it!

Group Piece Slam—The name says it all. In this slam you can only perform a poem with at least one other person. It can be a duet or quintet, but it can't be performed by only one person.

(Insert Topic Here) Slam—Are you studying the Civil War? Have a Civil War Slam! Is it Women's History Month? Have a Women's History Month Slam! Science teacher Tim Bernier once staged a Periodic Table of Elements Slam. You can tailor a slam to any topic of study. Just give your students a topic or theme to write about.

A poetry slam is not a sacred event to be reserved for special occasions. It was made for all people to enjoy. Manipulate the form until you find a slam that will be entertaining and educational for your learning community.

GUIDELINES TO GOOD PERFORMANCE

1. *Be familiar enough with your poem to communicate the poems. This means making eye contact with the audience and delivering the lines of the poem in a smooth fashion.*

2. *Use emotion and inflection in your delivery. Also, if your poem has tempo changes, make sure you take note of it in your delivery. This does not mean reciting a mile a minute. It means choosing a tempo that helps the audience understand what you have to say.*

3. *Please make sure that you breathe. Do not run out of air mid-line. Run through the poems enough times so that you know where to breathe. Make notes for those places on your copy of the poem.*

4. *While standing to perform, do not lock your knees. It prevents the blood from circulating properly. It could wind up making you dizzy and lightheaded.*

5. *Deliver the poem with excellent volume and articulation. If we cannot hear you, we cannot understand you. Period. To have good articulation, warm up with a tongue twister or two. As cold as it is outside, the joints and muscles in our mouths and throats get stiff and creaky. Warm them up. Here are some tongue twisters to help. These also remind you to watch out for repetition of sounds in the writing.*

Red leather—Yellow leather—Good blood—Bad blood

Unique New York. New York unique. You know you need unique New York

The Lethe police dismisseth us.

What a to-do to die today at a minute or two to two
A thing distinctly hard to say but harder still to do
For they'll beat a tattoo at twenty to two a rat-tat-tat-tat-tat-tat-tat-tat-too
And the dragon will come when he hears the drum
At a minute or two to two today. At a minute or two to two.

Peter Piper picked a peck of pickled peppers.

Theophilus Thistle, the successful thistle sifter, in sifting a sieve full of unsifted thistles, thrust three thousand thistles through the thick of his thumb.

Mamma made me mash my M&Ms.

Amidst the mists and coldest frosts/With stoutest wrists and loudest boasts/He thrusts his fists against the posts/And still insists he sees the ghosts.

COUNTDOWN TO PERFORMANCE

Ask yourself the following questions:

Have I…

- *Looked up any words I don't know or understand well in the poem?*

- *Asked for help if I don't fully understand what the poem's saying?*

- *Given consideration to the tempo of the poem?*

- *Thought about the emotional tone of the piece?*

- *Noticed if it changes tone or tempo?*

- *Identified who the speaker of the poem is for my performance?*

- *Thought about how to "stage" the performance (gestures, body movement)?*

- *Practiced saying the poem aloud so that the delivery is smooth?*

- *Practiced enough so that I have great volume and articulation?*

- *Decided whether or not pauses help to communicate meaning in the poem?*

PERFORMANCE POETRY RUBRIC

Poet: _____ Name: _____

Poem: _____

	Outstanding	Solid	Adequate, but Uninspired	Absent
Volume & Articulation (smooth delivery of the poem)				
Communication of the poem (understanding the poem and able to convey meaning/ emotion to the audience)				
Staging the poem (gestures, movement, body language and tempo of poem)				
Fits requirements (G-rated poem, from the books or teacher approved, length)				
Creativity				

POETRY RUBRIC

Poet: _____   Name: _____

Poem: _____

	Outstanding	Solid	Adequate, but Uninspired	Absent
Use of figurative language or method being taught				
Follows the requirements of the poetic form (syllables, rhyme, meter, etc.)				
Uses sensory details to "show" and not "tell"				
Creativity				

STATE STANDARDS:

ILLINOIS STANDARDS

ISBE State Goals and Standards

Reading: Goal 1	Middle School:	Early High School:	Late High School:
Vocabulary:	1.A.3a	1.A.4a, 1.A.4b	1.A.5a, 1.A.5b
Reading Strategies:	1.B.3a, 1.B.3c, 1.B.3d	1.B.4a, 1.B.4b, 1.B.4c	1.B.5a, 1.B.5b, 1.B.5d
Comprehension:	1.C.3a, 1.C.3d, 1.C.3e	1.C.4a, 1.C.4b, 1.C.4c, 1.C.4d, 1.C.4e	1.C.5a, 1.C.5b, 1.C.5c, 1.C.5d

Literature: Goal 2	Middle School:	Early High School:	Late High School:
Literary Elements:	2.A.3a, 2.A.3b, 2.A.3c, 2.A.3d	2.A.4a, 2.A.4b, 2.A.4c, 2.A.4d	2.A.5a, 2.A.5b, 2.A.5c, 2.A.5d
Interpretation:	2.B.3a, 2.B.3b, 2.B.3c	2.B.4a, 2.B.4b, 2.B.4c	2.B.5a, 2.B.5b

Writing: Goal 3	Middle School:	Early High School:	Late High School:
Grammar:	3.A.3	3.A.4	3.A.5
Organized Writing:	3.B.3a, 3.B.3b	3.B.4a, 3.B.4b, 3.B.4c	3.B.5
Communicate Ideas:	3.C.3a, 3.C.3b	3.C.4a, 3.C.4b	3.C.5a, 3.C.5b

FLORIDA STANDARDS

Benchmarks: Language Arts

Reading Process:

Grade	Fluency	Vocabulary Development	Reading Comprehension
7	LA.7.1.5.1	LA.7.1.6.1, LA.7.1.6.2, LA.7.1.6.3, LA.7.1.6.6, LA.7.1.6.8, LA.7.1.6.9	LA.7.1.7.1, LA.7.1.7.2, LA.7.1.7.3, LA.7.1.7.6, LA.7.1.7.8
8	LA.8.1.5.1	LA.8.1.6.1, LA.8.1.6.2, LA.8.1.6.3, LA.8.1.6.5, LA.8.1.6.6, LA.8.1.6.8, LA.8.1.6.9	LA.8.1.7.1, LA.8.1.7.2, LA.8.1.7.3, LA.8.1.7.5, LA.8.1.7.6, LA.8.1.7.7
9, 10	LA.910.1.5.1	LA.910.1.6.1, LA.910.1.6.2, LA.910.1.6.3, LA.910.1.6.5, LA.910.1.6.6, LA.910.1.6.8, LA.910.1.6.9, LA.910.1.6.11	LA.910.1.7.1, LA.910.1.7.2, LA.910.1.7.3, LA.910.1.7.5, LA.910.1.7.6, LA.910.1.7.7
11,12	LA.1112.1.5.1	LA.1112.1.6.1, LA.1112.1.6.2, LA.1112.1.6.3, LA.1112.1.6.5, LA.1112.1.6.6, LA.1112.1.6.8, LA.1112.1.6.9	LA.1112.1.7.1, LA.1112.1.7.2, LA.1112.1.7.3, LA.1112.1.7.5, LA.1112.1.7.6, LA.1112.1.7.7

Writing Process:

Grade	Prewriting	Drafting	Revising & Editing Language Conventions	Publishing:
7	LA.7.3.1.1, LA.7.3.1.2	LA.7.3.2.3	LA.7.3.3.1, LA.7.3.3.3, LA.7.3.4.1, LA.7.3.4.2, LA.7.3.4.5	LA.7.3.5.1, LA.7.3.5.3
8	LA.8.3.1.1, LA.8.3.1.2	LA.8.3.2.2, LA.8.3.2.3	LA.8.3.3.1, LA.8.3.3.2, LA.8.3.3.3, LA.8.3.4.1, LA.8.3.4.3, LA.8.3.4.4, LA.8.3.4.5	LA.8.3.5.1, LA.8.3.5.3
9, 10	LA.910.3.1.1, LA.910.3.1.2	LA.910.3.2.2, LA.910.3.2.3	LA.910.3.3.1, LA.910.3.3.2, LA.910.3.3.3, LA.910.3.3.4, LA.910.3.4.1, LA.910.3.4.3, LA.910.3.4.4, LA.910.3.4.5	LA.910.3.5.1, LA.910.3.5.3
11,12	LA.1112.3.1.1, LA.1112.3.1.2	LA.1112.3.2.1, LA.1112.3.2.2, LA.1112.3.2.3	LA.1112.3.3.1, LA.1112.3.3.2, LA.1112.3.3.3, LA.1112.3.3.4, LA.1112.3.4.2, LA.1112.3.4.3, LA.1112.3.4.4, LA.1112.3.4.5	LA.1112.3.5.1, LA.1112.3.5.3

Writing Applications:

Grade:	Creative
7	LA.7.4.1.1, LA.7.4.1.2
8	LA.8.4.1.1, LA.8.4.1.2
9,10	LA.910.4.1.1, LA.910.4.1.2
11,12	LA.1112.4.1.1, LA.1112.4.1.2

ACKNOWLEDGMENTS

Tim Stafford would like to thank the teachers who took early looks at this collection of poetry, especially Dana Lord and Tim Bernier. He would also like to thank his students for being guinea pigs for most of these lessons.

Molly Meacham would like to thank Dr. Dagny Bloland, Molly's mentor teacher, for her contribution of the poetry log and her continued support. She would also like to thank Reina Hardy and Ellie Kaufman of The Viola Project for their outstanding creativity.

ABOUT THE AUTHORS

Tim Stafford is a poet and public school teacher from Chicago. He is the only poet to simultaneously hold the titles of "Chicago Slam Champion" and "World's Greatest Uncle." His work has appeared nationally on *HBO Def Poetry Jam*, *Borders Open Door Poetry*, and Chicago Public Radio. Internationally he has appeared at the ABC Brecht Festival in Augsburg, Germany and at the Munich Literature House. He can also be found performing as one half of the poetry duo "Death From Below," as one fifth of the "Speak'Easy Ensemble" directed by slam founder Marc Smith, and as a regular contributor to the critically acclaimed "Encyclopedia Show." He lives with his wife Dana, a yoga instructor and fellow public school teacher, and their dog Betsy.

Molly Meacham left her Tennessee home to avoid an MRS degree and wound up in Chicago studying theatre and poetry. She is a member of the Speak'Easy Poetry Ensemble directed by slam founder Marc Smith. They performed in Germany for the Bertolt Brecht Festival and at the Munich Literature House. Molly has performed on several stages in Australia, including on the RRR radio station. She also co-wrote and performed a commercial for the Big Ten. She has had poems published with journals including *Dew on the Kudzu*, *Bestiary Magazine*, *The Foundling Review*, and *Right Hand Pointing*. She teaches in a Chicago public school during the rest of her time.

WB 2011 LINEUP

38 BAR BLUES
New poems by CR Avery

WORKIN' MIME TO FIVE
Humor by Derrick Brown

YESTERDAY WON'T GOODBYE
New poems by Brian Ellis

THESE ARE THE BREAKS
New prose & poetry by Idris Goodwin

THE FEATHER ROOM
New poems by Anis Mojgani

LOVE IN A TIME OF ROBOT APOCALYPSE
New poems by David Perez

THE UNDISPUTED GREATEST WRITER OF ALL TIME
New poems by Beau Sia

SUNSET AT THE TEMPLE OF OLIVES
New poems by Paul Suntup

GENTLEMAN PRACTICE
New poems by Buddy Wakefield

HOW TO SEDUCE A WHITE BOY IN TEN EASY STEPS
New poems by Laura Yes Yes

THE NEW CLEAN
New poems by Jon Sands

BRING DOWN THE CHANDELIERS
New poems by Tara Hardy

WRITE ABOUT AN EMPTY BIRDCAGE
New poems by Elaina M. Ellis

REASONS TO LEAVE THE SLAUGHTER
New poems by Ben Clark

OTHER WRITE BLOODY BOOKS

EVERYTHING IS EVERYTHING (2010)
New poems by Cristin O'Keefe Aptowicz

DEAR FUTURE BOYFRIEND (2010)
A Write Bloody reissue of Cristin O'Keefe Aptowicz's first book of poetry

HOT TEEN SLUT (2010)
A Write Bloody reissue of Cristin O'Keefe Aptowicz's second book of poetry
about her time writing for porn

WORKING CLASS REPRESENT (2010)
A Write Bloody reissue of Cristin O'Keefe Aptowicz's third book of poetry

OH, TERRIBLE YOUTH (2010)
A Write Bloody reissue of Cristin O'Keefe Aptowicz's fourth book of poetry
about her terrible youth

CATACOMB CONFETTI (2010)
New poems by Josh Boyd

THE BONES BELOW (2010)
New poems by Sierra DeMulder

CEREMONY FOR THE CHOKING GHOST (2010)
New poems by Karen Finneyfrock

MILES OF HALLELUJAH (2010)
New poems by Rob "Ratpack Slim" Sturma

RACING HUMMINGBIRDS (2010)
New poems by Jeanann Verlee

YOU BELONG EVERYWHERE (2010)
Road memoir and how-to guide for travelling artists

LEARN THEN BURN (2010)
Anthology of poems for the classroom. Edited by Tim Stafford and Derrick Brown.

STEVE ABEE, GREAT BALLS OF FLOWERS (2009)
New poems by Steve Abee

SCANDALABRA (2009)
New poetry compilation by Derrick Brown

DON'T SMELL THE FLOSS (2009)
New Short Fiction Pieces By Matty Byloos

THE LAST TIME AS WE ARE (2009)
New poems by Taylor Mali

IN SEARCH OF MIDNIGHT: THE MIKE MCGEE HANDBOOK OF AWESOME (2009)
New poems by Mike McGee

ANIMAL BALLISTICS (2009)
New poems by Sarah Morgan

CAST YOUR EYES LIKE RIVERSTONES INTO THE EXQUISITE DARK (2009)
New poems by Danny Sherrard

SPIKING THE SUCKER PUNCH (2009)
New poems by Robbie Q. Telfer

THE GOOD THINGS ABOUT AMERICA (2009)
An illustrated, un-cynical look at our American Landscape. Various authors.
Edited by Kevin Staniec and Derrick Brown

THE ELEPHANT ENGINE HIGH DIVE REVIVAL (2009)
Anthology

PULL YOUR BOOKS UP BY THEIR BOOTSTRAPS

Write Bloody Publishing distributes and promotes great books of fiction, poetry and art every year. We are an independent press dedicated to quality literature and book design, with an office in Long Beach, CA.

Our employees are authors and artists so we call ourselves a family. Our design team comes from all over America: modern painters, photographers and rock album designers create book covers we're proud to be judged by.

We publish and promote 8-12 tour-savvy authors per year. We are grass-roots, D.I.Y., bootstrap believers. Pull up a good book and join the family. Support independent authors, artists and presses.

Visit us online:

WRITEBLOODY.com

Lightning Source UK Ltd.
Milton Keynes UK
UKHW030703271220
375899UK00012B/1459